WEST CHESHIRE
walks

- from Warrington to Whitchurch
Wilmslow to the Wirral

by

Jen Darling

Sigma Leisure - Wilmslow

First published in 1988   Reprinted in 1990, 1991, 1995, 2000
Sigma Press 1 South Oak Lane, Wilmslow, SK9 6AR, England.

Publisher's Note

While every effort has been made to ensure that the information given in this book is correct, the publishers do not accept responsibility for any inaccuracy.

British Library Cataloguing in Publication Data

Darling, J.M. (Jennifer M.)
    West Cheshire walks.
    1. West Cheshire. Visitors' guides
    914.27'104858

ISBN: 1-85058-111-8

Cover design by Colin Ellis

Cover photograph by Graham Beech

Picture Acknowledgements:

London Bridge Pub, Daresbury Lane - to Jack Gregory.

Australia Lane, Grappenhall - to 'Brentwood Arts'.

Elizabethan Farmhouse - to Jonathan Morris.

Anderton Boat Lift - to Graham Beech

Printed in Great Britain by
MFP Design & Print, Longford Trading Est., Thomas St., Manchester M32 0JT.

FOREWORD

Mrs Darling is to be warmly complimented on presenting us with this excellent book of walks using our local footpaths. There is much talk of increased leisure in the countryside, and there is no better way to enjoy yourself than by making full use of our traditional rights to walk field footpaths.

In my pre-war youth it was commonplace for young and old to take such walks after church on Sunday evening, and our local footpaths were then pleasantly busy with folk enjoying the countryside in this most relaxing of ways.

Largely through disuse, many of these footpaths are no longer "walkable", and it would be a tragedy if we lost our age-old rights to use them.

I urge you to use Mrs Darling's book and walk the paths which she describes in great detail. By so doing your eyes will be opened to our greatest and perhaps most fragile heritage - our lovely English countryside.

Joseph Lythgoe,

Chairman, Council for the Protection of Rural England (Cheshire Branch).

Unusual stile on the Alvanley walk.

PREFACE

West Cheshire Walks contains 40 walks of varying lengths, with a sketchmap for each route. The walks are suitable for the lone walker, groups, families and dogs, and the author hopes it will have something to suite all tastes. It has been written as a companion volume to the book *East Cheshire Walks* - also from Sigma Leisure - now in its second edition.

Many of the walks in the sections nearest to Warrington are short as they were originally written for a book entitled 'Sunday Strolls', devised as a pleasant alternative to falling asleep in front of the T.V. after Sunday dinner! However, the book has 'growed' (like Topsy!) and so has the area covered. I suppose, in a sense, I sent details of my original manuscript to the publisher at the right time - when 'East Cheshire Walks' was selling well.

I have given travelling instructions for each walk from the nearest large town, and have tried to suggest parking places off the road wherever possible. All the walks are circular. I have not mentioned bus and train times as these seem to alter so frequently the information could well be inaccurate before the book is published.

The lengths of the walks are approximate. The time it takes to do them will vary depending on the terrain and the people involved. As a rough guide, I usually reckon to walk between two to three miles per hour - and my family tell me I am slow! Much of the landscape covered by the walks could be described as gently undulating. There are one or two pulls up to higher ground where you might get slightly puffed, for instance on the Primrose Hill and Raw Head routes, but there is nothing severe.

There are many places worth visiting for those on holiday in the area, and I have mentioned these in the introduction to each section. Some of the shorter walks could easily be combined with a visit to the nearest one.

I should like to thank all those who have helped me with this book in any way - however unwittingly! Particular thanks are due to Alan Miller for his persistent encouragement in the beginning, to Tom Carding for the use of his dictaphone, and to Valerie West for help with publicity and for the many times she has sat and listened to me wittering on! Thanks are also due to my family - for putting up with the way I don't listen to what they say! And, of course, to the publisher - for giving me a contract!

Please contact me if you have any information that may be useful for future editions of this book.

Have fun!

Jen Darling

CONTENTS

INTRODUCTION

The aim of this book is to encourage people to enjoy walking in some of the pretty countryside of Cheshire. I have tried to use footpaths and bridleways as much as possible rather than roads, to add interest to the routes.

Below I have attempted to give a small insight into the many facets that make up the 'flavour' of the region. Some of these characteristics occur in many of the walks.

History

There is evidence of settlement in the area from early times. This is shown in the iron age forts, for example Woodhouse hill fort near Frodsham and Maiden Castle further south.

Chester was an important Roman settlement and fortress. Its Roman name was Deva. Northwich and Middlewich too date from that time when the former was called Condate and the latter Salinae - the Latin word for salt. Watling Street was the Roman road linking the garrison at Chester with the fort of Mamucium (Manchester), and King Street, which goes from Northwich down to Middlewich and beyond, is also Roman.

Runcorn also dates from Roman times. The ruins of Halton Castle, built in the 12th century to defend the river approaches, can still be seen above the town. However, the best example of a castle in Cheshire is Beeston.

Industry

One large area of industry is in the north of the area along the Mersey. The Stanlow Oil Refinery was established near Ellesmere Port by Shell in 1924. It still uses canal water for cooling purposes. The massive cooling towers of Fiddlers Ferry Power Station, on the outskirts of Widnes, dominate the northern skyline too.

The salt industry grew around the towns known as the three 'wiches' - Northwich, Nantwich and Middlewich - and around Winsford. The ICI has huge works near Northwich, where it originally had its roots in salt.

It now manufactures chemicals and has other bases at Runcorn and Widnes.

Waterways

Rivers and canals feature in many of the walks.

Rivers

The River Mersey formed the natural boundary between Lancashire and Cheshire until Widnes and Warrington were moved into Cheshire to increase both the industry and the population of the county! The Mersey is navigable for 19 miles from its estuary at Liverpool to Warrington. The steel suspension bridge that joins Widnes to Runcorn is an attractive sight from high ground on some of the walks. When it was completed in 1961 it was the longest in Europe and was built to replace the earlier transporter bridge.

There is an old Cheshire rhyme which says:

'The Weaver, the Peover, the Wheelock and Dane,
When they all meet together they change their name.'
- They all run into the Mersey.

The River Weaver is completely in Cheshire. It rises close to the village of Peckforton and enters the River Mersey near Frodsham. It was made navigable in the 18th century to carry salt from Nantwich, Winsford and Northwich to the docks at Runcorn for export. All the locks along its course are manned by keepers, but road transport has taken much of its trade.

The smaller rivers of the Dane and the Peover Eye feature in walks, as does the River Gowy as it wanders around the countryside.

Canals

Here are one or two things to look out for when walking along the towpaths of the canals that form such a network through the Cheshire countryside. Spare balance beams and stop planks (used when the locks are drained for repairs) are to be found near many locks. They are often protected from the weather by a roof, or are in a special chamber under a bridge. The curved path, often made of brick, with foot-stops for easy purchase is another feature to be found at locks. And, of course, there is

2

the lock-keeper's cottage, sometimes with a small-holding attached.

The Manchester Ship Canal can be seen from high ground on several of the walks. It is almost 37 miles long with five locks. Queen Victoria opened it in 1894 and sailed up its length from Liverpool to Manchester. It was directly responsible for making Manchester into one of Britain's largest seaports, despite being 32 miles from the coast. An enormous amount of industry has grown up on the banks of this canal. It also has some of the largest swing bridges, for instance, the three to the south of Warrington. The rival to these is over the Weaver a little further south on the A49 at Acton Bridge.

The Bridgewater Canal was the first canal to be built in England. It extends for 28 miles from Worsley near Manchester to Runcorn in Cheshire, where it used to enter the River Mersey via a series of locks. It was designed by the famous engineer James Brindley and was opened in 1765.

It was built to distribute coal from Worsley, but it also had other uses. It transported raw cotton from Liverpool to Manchester, and a passenger service operated to take people to Manchester. Two of the stopping points were Stockton Heath and Lymm, and the fare was 1d per mile! Nowadays, the canal is used by pleasure craft and fishermen and its towpath provides an interesting section to several of the walks.

When the Trent and Mersey was being built it was known as the Grand Trunk Canal. James Brindley designed this canal but died before it was completed. Josiah Wedgwood, of pottery fame, backed it as did the Duke of Bridgewater, and its function was to join the Potteries to the Mersey and Manchester. One of its functions was to transport china clay which came up to Liverpool from Cornwall.

This canal is 93 miles long and it runs from Preston Brook to the River Trent at Shardlow. The cast-iron, two-armed mileposts along its bank give the distance between these two places. They date from about 1819. This canal was built to take wide beam boats. The Saltersford Tunnel, which you visit on the Little Leigh walk, was one of the first major canal tunnels to be constructed.

The Shropshire Union Canal links Ellesmere Port with Wolverhampton and is 66 miles long. The engineer responsible for all the section in Cheshire was Thomas Telford. It was originally planned in three sections, the Chester to Nantwich part being known as the Chester Canal. It has some interesting features. The one-roomed, round buildings at Tilston and Beeston locks are huts where the lock keeper sheltered. He would brew tea there and sleep if on night duty.

The Countryside

Parks and Meres

Cheshire is often described as a region of parks and meres. Much of the parkland belongs to estates that have been owned by families for generations. Examples of these are the Grosvenor estate at Eaton Hall, near Chester, and the Tatton estate which was owned by the Egerton family until the National Trust took it over. The estate villages and tenant farms are always well-maintained and often have distinctive characteristics.

There are many meres, both natural and man-made. Rostherne is the largest natural one, while the ones around Northwich have been caused by salt mining and are known as 'flashes'. 'Mosses' are another common phenomena where peaty ground has formed woodland or marshes.

Houses

Georgian houses, as at Christleton, were made of bricks from local clay found on the Cheshire Plain. Red sandstone was also quarried to provide building material for houses and bridges, and there are many of these still surviving.

Many houses and cottages in Cheshire are faced with white plaster inset by black beams of oak. These are often referred to as 'magpie' buildings and some of them are very old. There are many examples of these in the picturesque villages of Peckforton and Beeston, but you will notice them dotted all over the countryside. Many cottages still have their thatched roofs too.

Churches

Most of the villages are dominated by their church. Examples of these are the perpendicular designs of Great Budworth and Bunbury, and the soaring spire at Walton. Daresbury has its connection with Lewis Carroll, and High Legh boasts two churches of vastly differing design.

Farms

The rich pastureland of the plain is the reason for the many dairy farms in the area. Herds of Friesians predominate. Cheshire cheese used to be made on the farms, but most of this is now made in factories. Farm buildings, grouped in rectangles, still survive from the 18th and 19th centuries.

Sunken lanes and hedges

Cheshire is noted for lanes that have high banks on either side, often topped by hedges. Hawthorn is the main material used for hedges throughout the area. As children we used to call this 'bread and cheese' and we would nibble surreptiously at the leaves to see if they really tasted of this. Well-established hedges round fields will often have trees, particularly oaks, growing from them at intervals. These provide shade and shelter for cattle, and nesting places for birds.

Marl Pits

In many fields in Cheshire there is a pond for watering cattle. Some of these areas used to have deposits of a black clay called 'marl'. This was dug out and spread over the rest of the field to enrich the sandy soil. Gangs of men used to go from farm to farm to dig up this marl and spread it. They were known as 'marlers', and the dip in the ground left behind filled up with rainwater and became known as a marl pit.

The Sandstone Trail

A sandstone ridge intermittently bisects the Cheshire plain from north to south, starting from Beacon Hill above Frodsham and ending near Whitchurch. The Trail follows this ridge and is 30 miles. Several of the walks cover part of it. It passes through a variety of scenery, from the Overton Hills around Frodsham, through Delamere Forest, to the craggy hills around Raw Head, which is the highest point. It finally ends on the lush pastureland of the plain. You will see the distinctive trail markers of a footprint engraved with the letter 'S' along its route.

I hope that this introduction will give you a little knowledge of the rich heritage that our ancestors left behind for us to enjoy.

EQUIPMENT

There is very little equipment that you need in order to tackle these walks. I have found from experience that it is best to travel as light as possible. Here is a checklist before you start out.

A map In the introduction to each section I have given details of the Ordnance Survey Map that I have used. In each case it is one of the Pathfinder Series of Great Britain (1:25000). These are ideal for walkers as they give so much detail, even down to field boundaries. I would advise you to invest in the appropriate one before venturing forth if you can. Although I have tried to make the instructions as clear as possible, sometimes the countryside is altered - signs get moved or new roads are built. I am also human, and what might seem clear to me may be interpreted differently by someone else.

Footwear Boots are best but wellingtons or trainers are possible. Nylon socks are inadvisable as they cause blisters. I wear a pair of cotton socks and a pair of wool ones with boots. Some areas around field entrances where cows are tramping in and out get extremely mucky and it's not always possible to go round them.

Waterproofs An anorak or cagoule is advisable to cope with the vagaries of the British climate.

Sweaters A warm sweater, or two if it is winter. It is better to start off warm and then shed clothes. The nice thing about walking as a hobby, or just for pleasure occasionally, is that it doesn't matter what you look like! If you get hot, you can always sling a sweater round your waist.

Money A small amount of loose change is handy in case you spot a likely place for liquid refreshment!

Miscellaneous It is best to carry as little as possible but you may want to take a small rucksack for oddments like plasters and food. I have a coat with voluminous pockets in which to stuff apple, cheese and chocolate, and I leave a thermos of hot water with coffee and milk in the car.

There is little gradient work, so you won't need ropes or crampons!

THE COUNTRY CODE

Enjoy the countryside, but respect its life and work.
Fasten all gates.
Keep to public paths across farmland.
Use gates and stiles to cross fences, hedges and walls.
Go carefully on country roads.
Leave no litter.
Protect all wild life, plants and trees.
Help to keep all water clean.
Guard against all risk of fire.
Make no unnecessary noise.
Leave livestock, crops and machinery alone.
Keep dogs under close control.

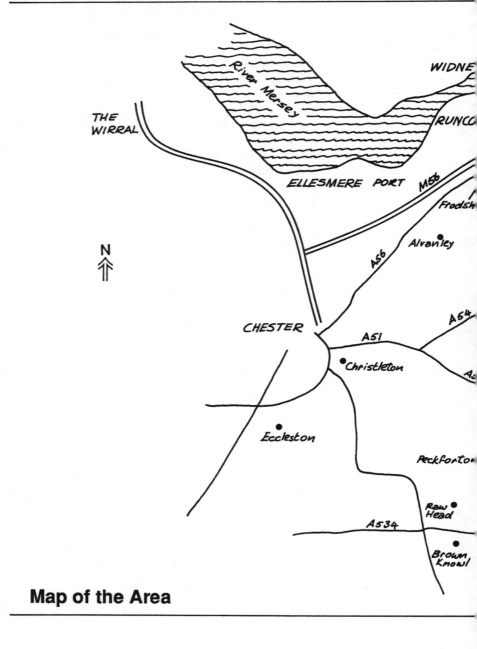

Map of the Area

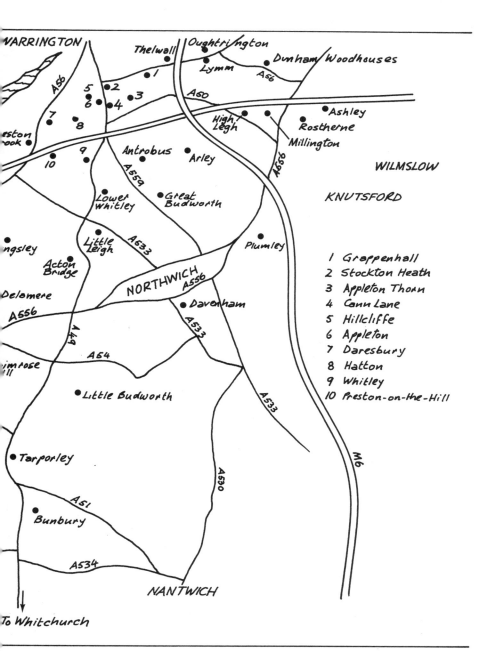

WARRINGTON

Thelwall   Oughtrington
Lymm   Dunham Woodhouses
A56   A56

A56

5   2   3
6   4

7
8   High
Legh   Ashley
Rostherne
Millington

ston
ook
9   Antrobus   Arley   A5656   WILMSLOW
10   A559   KNUTSFORD

Lower
Whitley   Great
Budworth

ngsley   Little
Leigh   A533   Plumley   1 Grappenhall
Acton
Bridge   2 Stockton Heath
Delamere   NORTHWICH   A556   3 Appleton Thorn
A556   4 Cann Lane
A49   Davenham   5 Hillcliffe
6 Appleton
imrose
ll   A54   A533   7 Daresbury
8 Hatton
Little Budworth   9 Whitley
10 Preston-on-the-Hill

Tarporley   A530   M6

A51

Bunbury

A534

NANTWICH

To Whitchurch

KEY

x	start/finish of walk
→	route
– – – – – – –	footpath
꞊꞊꞊꞊꞊꞊꞊	bridleway/private road
⸺	country lane
═══════	main road/motorway
+++++++	railway
⬭	lake
═══════	canal
∿∿∿∿	river/stream
♀♀⚲⚲	woodland
''' ''' '''	marsh
✝	church
■	building

All maps are to a scale of 1:25000.

SOUTH OF WARRINGTON

Appleton
Appleton Thorn
Cann Lane (Appleton)
Grappenhall
Hill Cliffe
Norcott Brook
Stockton Heath
Thelwall

The map in the Pathfinder series that covers these walks is Warrington - Sheet SJ68/78. The travelling instructions are given from Warrington. The walks are all two to three miles long and take between one and two hours to complete. However, several of them can be joined together to give longer walks.

For newcomers to the area, a visit to Walton Hall Gardens could be combined with any of the walks. There is a magnificent display of rhododendrons in the late spring. A playground and a miniature zoo keep youngsters happy, and a bowling green, crazy golf, and a miniature golf course are other attractions.

Each of the villages has its Walking Day in June or July. This ancient custom originated from the time when people used to walk round the boundaries of their land on a certain day. Nowadays, the afternoon usually begins with a short Church service followed by a procession, when local people run into the road to give the children coins to spend on the fair later.

AROUND APPLETON

Route: Dudlow Green Road - Pewterspear - Hillside Road - Golf Course - Firs Lane - Quarry Lane - London Road - Fairways - Pineways

Distance: 2 to 3 miles

Start: Parade of shops in Dudlow Green Road (SJ 623845)

By Car: Take the A49 south from Warrington and, after passing Warrington Golf Club on your right, turn left into Dudlow Green Road. (It is signposted to Appleton Parish Hall.) There is a large car-park behind the shops on this road.

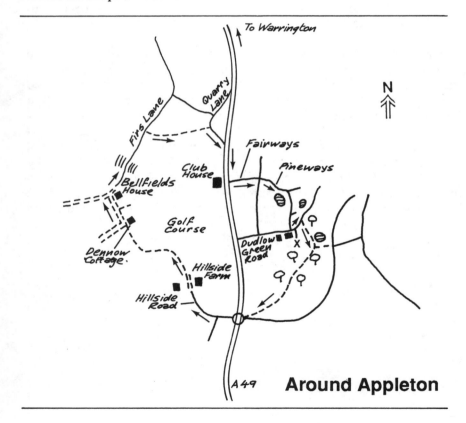

Around Appleton

Walk back onto Dudlow Green Road. Turn right and immediately right again down a footpath just before the first house. When you reach a bridleway turn right again and look out for grey squirrels. Continue through an avenue of beech trees, a delight to crunch through the fallen leaves in autumn. Stretton Church can be easily seen from here. On a clear day seven counties can be seen from the top of the tower, and you may be able to hear the six bells as they ring out over the countryside.

On reaching the roundabout on the main road cross over into Hillside Road. At the end of this you pass through the gateway leading to Hillside Farm. The distinctive concrete tower that comes into view is an extension of Daresbury Nuclear Physics Laboratory. It was built in 1975, much to the disgust of local residents, and it houses a synchrotron radiation source. Fiddlers Ferry Power Station also features prominently here. Climb over two stiles and continue along a grassy track to Dennow Cottage.

St John's Church, Walton - 'a miniature cathedral'.

At this point you will get a glimpse of Appleton Reservoir and Walton Church spire. The latter is said to have the appearance of a miniature cathedral in its idyllic setting. The top of the spire is 130 feet from the ground, and the church was built by Sir Gilbert Greenall late in the 19th century at a cost of £10,000. In fact, the Greenall family still take an active interest in it.

Turn right into Firs Lane past Bellfields House. The road winds uphill through eerie, sandstone cliffs. Notice the horse trough let into the rocky wall - relic of a bygone age. Turn right down a public footpath after passing a small field. Keep the bungalows on your left all the way along here.

Turn right into Quarry Lane, which gets its name from the old sandstone quarry behind the houses on your left. This is now used by a rifle shooting club. Turn right again onto the A49 and take the next left turn down Fairways, opposite the entrance to Warrington Golf Club. Each time a member dies the flag on the clubhouse is flown at half-mast, so locals on the waiting list for membership watch hopefully!

Keep straight on into Pineways and enjoy the wildlife on the pond. Mallards, coots and moorhens are plentiful, and you may be lucky enough to see a tufted duck or heron. Perch and roach can also sometimes be spotted in the water. The shops and the end of your walk are now ahead.

AROUND APPLETON THORN

Route: B5356 - Wright's Green - Green Lane

Distance: 2 to 3 miles

Start: Junction of B5356 and New Lane (SJ 646842)

By Car: Take the A49 from Warrington and turn left at Stretton traffic lights along the B5356. Go through Appleton Thorn and park the car where New Lane comes in from the left.

Walk along the main road towards the M6 and turn left down a rutted track into a field. Keep along the side of the hedge past two small ponds and jump the deep ditch into the next field. Over to the left the highest part of Hill Cliffe can be seen, it is marked by a stone obelisk with four lions at its base. This is positioned above the golf course and is a favourite area for children sledging in winter.

Where the hedge ends, make a right-angled turn to the left! (I hope this isn't too confusing for mathematicians!) When you come to the pylon turn right in front of the fence covered with bracken, and keep it beside you as you walk down the field. Go through the gateway into the next field and immediately turn left into another field. Continue along here until you reach Lumb Brook Road and turn left. The small settlement beside you is called Wright's Green.

New Lane soon cuts off to the left, but you carry straight on and turn right through the entrance into the next field opposite Cheriton Cottage. Climb over the fence out of this field and turn left along the cart track. You pass a charming black and white cottage built in typical Cheshire style and dated 1630. Squeeze through the gap beside the gate and carry on along muddy Green Lane.

The thickets beside this road house a multitude of birds and eventually give way to a huge holly hedge, behind which the cackling of geese can be heard from the nearby farm. The towering mass of the Victorian vicarage looms into view ahead.

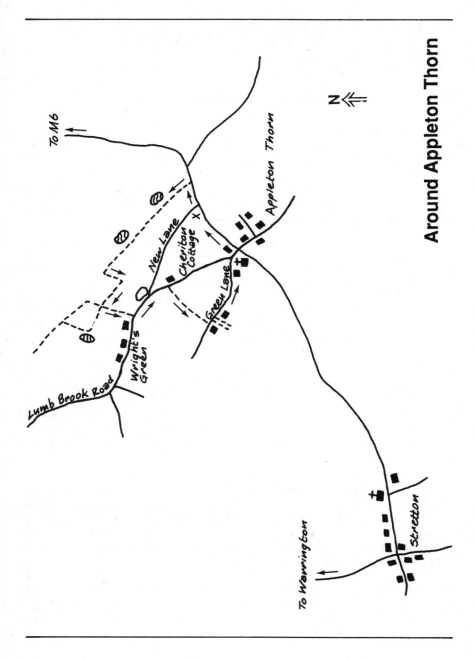

Around Appleton Thorn

Appleton Thorn Church was built in the late 19th century, like most of the churches in this area of similar design. Nearby stands the celebrated Thorn Tree. The original one is said to have been an offshoot of the Glastonbury Thorn, which is supposed to have grown from the staff of Joseph of Arimathea and to have bloomed at Christmas. This latest one is a recent cutting from the Glastonbury Thorn. Appleton Thorn is the only place in England where the ancient custom of 'Bawming the Thorn' is still continued. The word 'bawming' means 'adorning' or 'decorating' the tree with flowers or ribbons. The ceremony takes place each summer on Appleton Thorn Walking Day.

Turn left at the main road and pass the Thorn Inn. There is an interesting rhyme written on the lintel inside the porch door.

> "You may safely while sober sit under the Thorn
> But if drunk overnight it will prick you next morn."

You then pass Crofton Lodge, with the buildings of Appleton Thorn Youth Custody Centre behind it, before arriving back at your car.

AROUND CANN LANE

Route: Dudlow Green Road - Longwood Road - Dingle Lane - Green Lane - Cann Lane

Distance: 2 to 3 miles

Start: The parade of shops in Dudlow Green Road (SJ 623845)

By Car: Take the A49 south from Warrington. After passing Warrington Golf Club on your right take the next turn left into Dudlow Green Road. When you reach the Freezer Centre you will find a large car-park behind it.

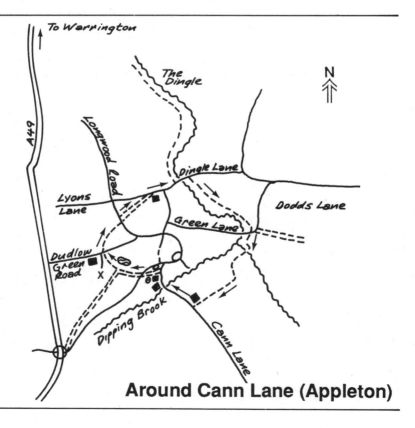

Around Cann Lane (Appleton)

Walk back onto Dudlow Green Road and turn right. You turn left almost immediately under the arch between the two blocks of retirement flats. Notice the traditional weather vane on the top of this building. Walk straight down through the attractive gardens and then along a grassy tract of land until you reach Longwood Road.

Turn left here, and then straightaway bear right onto a cart track. Walk to the white house ahead - the teenagers in the area are convinced that it is haunted! Here you will cross over Lyons Lane into Dingle Lane. Lyons Lane is named after a famous landowner in the area. He built the original Appleton Hall on the site where you may have glimpsed the large school over to your left. You may get a close look at grey squirrels here, and plenty of bird life can be seen and heard.

To the left is the Dingle, an area well worth exploring. But our walk today stays on the road as it crosses the brook. You then take the stile on the right-hand side of the road. Great care should be taken along this path as it can be extremely muddy, and the drop down to the stream is sheer in places. Large clumps of primroses and bluebells make this a very pretty place in springtime, with the stream burbling over tiny waterfalls.

Climb over the stile out of this miniature valley and turn right into Green Lane. The dulcet tones of the Appleton Thorn footballers may be heard in the distance! Ignore the bridleway that goes to the left, and go either over or under a rickety stile into a field. Walk along, keeping the stream on your right until you cross over it in the corner.

Climb over the shaky fence here and walk up the field to the top, keeping the electricity pylon on your right and the tree that marks the end of an obsolete hedge on your left. At the same time make for a wide oak tree in the top hedge. Turn right alongside this hedge and follow the cart-track which continues to the farmyard. Don't be alarmed by the noisy dogs, they are not loose. When you reach Cann Lane turn right.

As you walk down the road you will notice that Dipping Brook runs under it. At one time large stones were used to dam the stream here, so that a pool was made deep enough for baptismal immersions to take place.

After passing Brook House you soon turn left down a bridleway and almost immediately cross over a new road to continue along the track until it branches. At this point you take the right fork and pass a delightful area of wild woodland which used to be part of the Appleton Hall estate. Pear trees and rhododendrons still flourish here and before you reach the end of this path it becomes cobbled. On arriving back in Dudlow Green Road, turn left and return to the car-park.

AROUND GRAPPENHALL

Route: Broad Lane - Grappenhall Heys - Church Lane - Australia Lane

Distance: 2 to 3 miles

Start: Near Whitehouse Farm on Broad Lane (SJ 641856)

By Car: Take the A49 from Warrington. Turn left at Stretton traffic lights onto the B5356. Go through Appleton Thorn and turn left down Broad Lane. After passing Whitehouse Farm park on the grass verge which is fairly wide and flat.

Walk down the road, crossing the stream and turning left along Hall Lane as you breast the top of the slope. This soon becomes a grassy track and you will pass a small pond. Bear left into a field, hugging the hedge on your right until you reach a gate set into it. Climb over it and cross straight over the field ahead, keeping the derelict, brick structure on your right. The views to the north are quite stunning and there is a particularly clear view of the cantilever bridge over the Manchester Ship Canal.

Make for the gap in the facing hedge beside a small pond, but you will probably have to climb the iron fence. There is a faint line straight across the next field which you should follow. Turn right along the far hedge and keep going until you reach a small copse teeming with wildlife. Here you pass through a small iron gate into a field which may have heifers in it. The large herd of Friesian cows which are kept here at Dairy Farm may be providing you with some of the milk you drink each day.

Turn right up the field to join the track to Grappenhall Heys. This used to be a big house with extensive grounds. The original owner of the estate shut this track to the public on one day every year to prevent it being declared a public right of way. The swans and ducks bred on the pond can be both seen and heard. I was once lucky enough to see a heron rise from the field almost beside me.

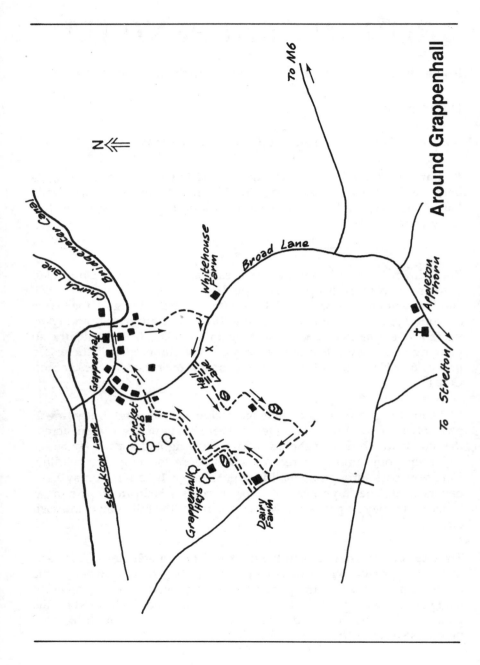

Around Grappenhall

The track turns right and you may pass a silage heap protected from the weather by a mass of car tyres. Go over the cattle grid, or through the handy gate at the side for the more sedate! Pass Grappenhall Cricket Club and the old lodge at the estate entrance to reach Broad Lane once more.

Cross straight over this and carry on along the footpath that skirts behind the houses. The Georgian hall over to your right is now a school. When you meet the road, which is Church Lane, turn right along the cobbled street. You will pass the primary school with its many extensions and come to the Ram's Head, which has an unusual sundial set into its sandstone facade.

The Parr Arms is the pub next to the Church and is the older of the two. The large orders from the bell-ringers often cause considerable confusion for the barmaids there! The ancient stocks outside the church are also a feature of the village. Apparently in the Middle Ages, at a certain time during the Sunday service, the churchwardens left the church and walked along the village street. Anyone found causing a

Australia Lane, Grappenhall.

disturbance was put in the stocks for the day. Even earlier than this, evidence has been found of a Bronze Age settlement at Grappenhall, and the font in the church may be of Saxon origin. The figure of a cat on the outside wall of the tower is said to be the one that gave Lewis Carroll his idea for the Cheshire Cat.

Continue past the church and when you reach the Bridgewater Canal turn right down Australia Lane. When the house aptly named Bridgewater faces you, turn right down a narrow path. This crosses a gushing stream and continues along the ridge of the field following the marching line of telegraph poles. Bear right at the facing hedge. The track continues to the road where you will see your car over to the right.

AROUND HILL CLIFFE

Route: Hill Cliffe - Park Lane - Appleton Reservoir - Houghs Lane - Hillfoot Farm - Red Lane

Distance: 2 to 3 miles

Start: The end of Windmill Lane above the cemetery (SJ 613850)

By Car: Take the A49 south from Warrington. After going up the hill out of Stockton Heath you pass a large school on your left. Take the next turn right up Quarry Lane, and the next right into Windmill Lane. Park at the end of Windmill Lane near the large cemetery.

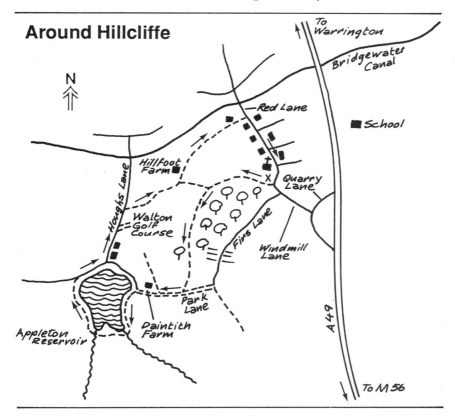

There are sweeping views of Warrington and the surrounding countryside from here and on a clear day you can easily see the Pennines. Follow the footpath sign to Walton Hall Gardens, going over the stile and along the side of the hill. The bulky mass on your left holds the underground storage reservoir that was constructed in the late 1960s. This can hold ten million gallons of water.

You will climb over two platform stiles along here and pass between clumps of gorse bushes and broom, ferns and bracken. You may also have an aerial view of games being played at Warrington Sports Club. Well-built wooden structures offer the newly-planted trees protection from horses. Squeeze through the opening at the side of the gate and pass a small plantation of evergreens and silver birches, where the land slopes down to Walton Golf Course; a municipal course open to anyone who fancies a game.

Pass some small oak trees and you come to an attractive picnic area, with a mass of rhododendrons providing a background of vivid colour in late spring. Keep on down the steps edged with logs to keep them firm. There is a double row of silver birches right along this broad ride, which brings you over the stile and into Firs Lane. Turn right along this rutted road.

Follow the signs to Appleton Reservoir walking down Park Lane past Daintith Farm. A Mr. Daintith was the second minister of Hill Cliffe Baptist Church, so the farm may have been named after him. The farmhouse is very picturesque, built of weathered sandstone slabs, probably quarried locally.

Go up the steps and onto the path round the reservoir. This was the original source of water for Warrington and was built in 1846. It still supplies Warrington with a million gallons of water a day for industrial use, and it must be a constant delight to both bird watchers and fishermen. Fly fishing is allowed and is very popular along the banks. Go round the end of the reservoir and back down the opposite bank. You do need to be fairly slim to squeeze through the openings in the fences!

Turn right when you reach the road again and then turn left down Houghs Lane, signposted Walton Hall Gardens. You might chuckle at the sign 'Caution, Golfers crossing ahead!' Take the turn after this to

Hillfoot Farm. The track by-passes the farm with its pretty, white-fronted farmhouse, and continues to Red Lane, which you enter between well-maintained hedgerows.

Turn right up the hill and you will come to Hill Cliffe Baptist Church, which may have been the first Baptist Church to be built. Cromwell is known to have worshipped here and one of the early ministers was a breadbaker in Bridge Street.

Continue on the path up through the ancient cemetery - a steady pull to end your walk. The gravestones get older as you go up the hill, and you may well feel older with them! The oldest authentic stone is dated 1664. Go through the large black and white lychgate to reach your car.

AROUND NORCOTT BROOK

Route: Queastybirch Hall - The Millstone - Grimsditch Hall - Raddel Lane - Dark Lane - Limes Lane

Distance: 2 to 3 miles

Start: Pillmoss Lane, Norcott Brook (SJ 613811)

By Car: Take the A49 from Warrington. When you come to the M56 roundabout continue along the A49. Take the next right turn - a very narrow opening - down Pillmoss Lane. Park your car in the small car park opposite the Methodist Church. This attractive black and white building with its rounded window tops was built in 1802.

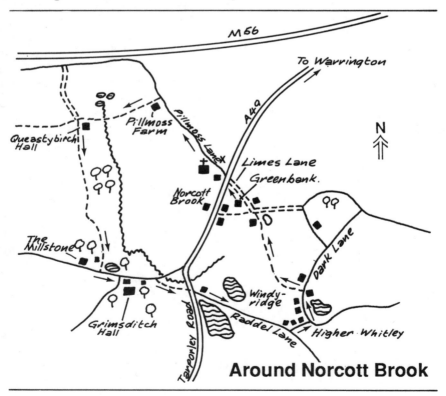

Around Norcott Brook

Whitley is a village divided into two parts - Higher Whitley and Lower Whitley. It is mentioned in a history book dated 1666 as being a township, and Cromwell camped at Lower Whitley with his army.

Walk down the country lane until you pass the second Pillmoss Farm, when you turn left through the farmyard and out onto a broad strip of grass between two fields. Continue over the stile and follow the telegraph poles to the stream, which you cross using a sturdy plank. You then keep ahead along the side of the field to Queastybirch Hall. Pass the first farm buildings, climb the stile and turn left.

Walk down between well-kept hawthorn hedges, and at the end of the second field (in front of the gate), bear left and walk along beside the hedge. Cross the stile here by some recent rabbit holes. The right of way then goes straight ahead across the field. Aim for the corner of the coppice, and you will arrive at a little path by a pond, which was used by Lymm Angling Club until pollution killed the fish. You will now arrive at a road. To your right 'The Millstone' public house serves food and drink.

However, you turn left along the road past Grimsditch Hall, hiding behind its high wall. It is one of the oldest buildings in the area, dating from 1666 when it was a small manor. Next, you will see the Brownie and Guide hut beside the wood. Go over the stile before the stream and walk alongside it for a short way before crossing the field to the stile in front of the white house.

Cross the busy Tarporley Road and go down Raddel Lane. A striking white house down here is called Morris Hill. It has black lintels over all the windows and the door. Pass water-filled quarries on either side of the road. You can see the primary school in the distance as you come into the village. One schoolmaster is remembered for having been able to write the whole of the Lord's Prayer on a piece of paper the size of a threepenny bit. At one time a local charity used to provide shoes for all the children attending the school.

Turn left towards Antrobus, Budworth and Northwich; and left again at the pond down Dark Lane, passing Mallard Cottage and several other attractive properties. Turn left through the gate into the field after you have passed Windyridge. If you get to Ashfield Mews, you have missed the turning. Last time I did this walk I think the owner of the field had forgotten that it was a public right of way as there was a strand of barbed wire fixed all round the field to keep in a shire horse.

Follow the garden hedge until it ends and then carry on across the field making for the spot where the telegraph poles meet the facing hedge. Go across the stream here and over the stile ahead. Keep the hedge on your left until you get to a pond and are greeted by the clacking of geese.

Turn left past Greenbank and walk down Limes Lane until you reach the A49. Facing you is Pillmoss Lane where you left your car.

AROUND STOCKTON HEATH

Route: Bridgewater Canal - The Dingle - Lyons Lane - Broomfields Road
- Delphfields Road - Birchdale Road

Distance: 2 to 3 miles

Start: Mitchell Street, near London Bridge (SJ 617858)

By Car: Take the A49 from Warrington and, after passing through
Stockton Heath, turn right down Mitchell Street just before you go over
London Bridge. Park anywhere in this area.

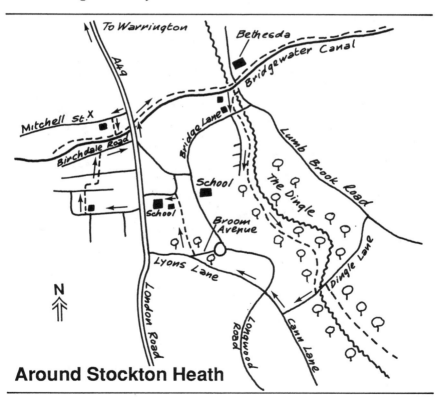

Around Stockton Heath

You can go down to the canal here beside the garage workshop. Walk under the wide, low arch of London Bridge and you will then get the best view of the pub of that name. In front of it is the steep flight of steps down to the canal where people boarded the fast passenger boats bound for Manchester in the 18th and 19th centuries. Walk along past pleasure boats and back gardens. You have a good view of the cantilever bridge along here, and of Warrington parish church which has one of the tallest church spires in the country. You may also see steam billowing out from the chimneys of Crosfield's soap factory.

London Bridge pub

To leave the towpath at Lumb Brook Bridge you go past the bridge and then double back. This aqueduct was built by Brindley and there is a record of road repairs pertaining to this bridge in an ancient ledger. The entry reads, '1737. Repairing Bridge at Lumb Brook 3s'. You wouldn't get much repair work done for that price nowadays! On your way down to the underbridge you pass Bethesda Chapel. This was opened in 1957 and in order to make the site big enough to take the foundations part of the canal bank had to be carved away.

Go under the bridge and continue down a rough sliproad in front of some houses. Cross over Bridge Lane and continue along a grassy tract. You keep Lumb Brook beside you right up its valley, passing Wood Lane and Hinton Crescent, and then continuing along a litter-strewn footpath and on into the pleasanter reaches of 'The Dingle' with its banks of rhododendrons and variety of trees and wild life.

Turn right when you come to Dingle Lane and then right again into Lyons Lane. As you will see the new road developments have sliced this road into three. Cross Longwood Road and continue along Lyons Lane. Then continue into Caversham Close. You will notice Broom Avenue on your right here and some wild areas that once formed an overgrown woodland garden. There used to be a Victorian house too called Broom Cottage and this spot is still referred to locally by that name. Continue down the footpath that separates the high school from the catholic primary school, and turn left into Broomfields Road.

When you reach London Road go straight across into Delphfields Road and continue along it until, after passing Cobweb Cottage at the end, you turn down a footpath alongside a beech hedge. This continues all the way down the hill and is known locally as 'The Rabbit Run'. The people that still live in the older houses on this estate can remember when the whole area was a grassy hill. Now they enjoy watching the children play instead of the rabbits!

When you reach Birchdale Road and can go no further downhill turn right and you will soon arrive back at London Bridge. Turn left over the bridge and return to your car.

AROUND THELWALL

Route: Weaste Lane - Bridgewater Canal - Lymm Road - Pickering Arms - Gig Lane - Woodlands Drive

Distance: 2 to 3 miles

Start: Weaste Lane, Thelwall (SJ 653865)

By Car: Take the A50 south from Warrington. After passing the 'Dog and Dart' in Grappenhall go straight on at the traffic lights towards the M6. Then turn left immediately into Cliff Road (signposted Massey Brook), and then left again into Weaste Lane. Park anywhere along this road after passing Oak Farm.

Walk along Weaste Lane until you see a stile and a footpath sign to the left. It is opposite an attractive white house fronted by a high beech hedge. Follow the tractor track across the field which eventually becomes a single file path and takes you over the Bridgewater Canal. This is Pickering Bridge and is named after a family who came to the area in 1662. Turn along the canal bank, walking past the boats moored along the far bank The semi-submerged craft surrounded by a mass of half-burnt rubbish gives the effect of sad dereliction.

Pass Thelwall Underbridge which takes Halfacre Lane under the canal. You come to a small wood here - a delightful spot for children to play. After passing a field turn left down a footpath. Vehicles, often of the decrepit variety, are piled up on either side of it, but it will bring you out into Dean's Lane where there is a bridge over the railway.

Turn right when you reach the main road, crossing over as soon as is safely possible, and then continue until you turn left along the old Lymm Road. You soon come to Old Hall Farm Shop. Falconry used to be a popular pastime at Old Hall Farm and the birds flew into the rafters of the house to roost there. Turn right into Laskey Lane and immediately left down a narrow footpath. After going through a little white gate cross the field diagonally, walking away from the road.

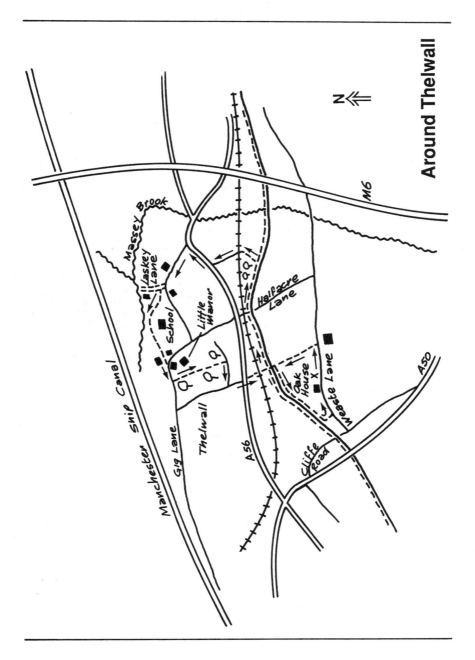

The path then continues through woodland beside a high wall, which is the boundary of Chaigeley School. This area is rather spoilt by man's unwanted litter but an attractive culvert of clear water runs out from under the wall and drops down to Massey Brook over clean paving stones.

The Pickering Arms and Thelwall village.

The path comes out at Thelwall Post Office and the Pickering Arms - a very ancient tavern. The writing on its gable end is a translation from an Anglo-Saxon Chronicle and states,

IN THE YEAR 923
KING EDWARD THE ELDER FOUNDED A CYTY HERE AND
CALLED IT THELWALL

Before the cutting of the Manchester Ship Canal the houses round here were subject to flooding and there is a tale that there was once enough flood water in the cellars of the Pickering Arms to put out a fire in the bakery at the Post Office opposite. Another source tells how a pig trough was used as a raft by the bakery to deliver the bread in floodtime. Nowadays, outside the Post Office is a map denoting the Thelwall Conservation Area and the Environment Project that is to be implemented here.

Keep straight on and then turn left into Gig Lane passing the back of 'The Little Manor'. An attractive park opens up along here with swings and roundabouts. Cross this and enter a passage flanked by an ornamental wall and wooden fence. On reaching the road turn right and when you come to the end of Woodlands Drive turn left, cross the main road and go down the track opposite.

Cross the railway and then the canal. Then turn right along the canal. The path meanders along the bank until you cross a stile and turn left between two fields. This brings you back to Weaste Lane. Turn left along here and walk back to your car.

NORTH OF KNUTSFORD

Ashley
Dunham Woodhouses
High Legh
Lymm
Millington
Oughtrington
Rostherne

The Pathfinder map for this area is Warrington - Sheet SJ68/78. All the travelling instructions are given from Warrington. Apart from the one near Ashley, the walks are all two to three miles in length and will take one to two hours to complete. Ashley is about five miles long and will probably take two or three hours to walk.

For visitors to the area, a trip to Dunham Massey Park could be combined with the walks around Lymm, Oughtrington or Dunham Woodhouses. The latter walk actually skirts the edge of this deer park.

The large Tatton Hall estate on the outskirts of Knutsford borders the other walks and offers a large variety of attractions. It is owned by the National Trust and a visit to the house gives you a look at life 'below stairs', in addition to viewing the stately rooms once occupied by the gentry. The gardens are splendid and there is extensive parkland. There is also a restored farm to see, and if you have a dinghy you can sail it on Tatton Mere.

AROUND ASHLEY

Route: Birkinheath Covert - M56 - River Bollin - Bowdon - Ashley Heath - Tatton Park Estate - Ashley Cricket Club - Lamb Lane

Distance : 5 miles

Start: Birkinheath Covert (SJ 761836)

By Car: Take the A49 from Warrington and turn left onto the M56. Take the Altrincham turn off the motorway (Junction 7) and follow the A556 towards Northwich which takes you back over the motorway. You then turn immediately left to Ashley. Keep left when you come to a T-junction which forks right for Rostherne. Park in the lay-by at the side of the road as you approach Birkinheath Covert.

It is tempting not to start this walk. Birdwatchers put food into the tins provided on top of posts here and there is a wealth of birdlife to watch. Some of the species you may see are: many varieties of the tit family, jays, nuthatches and woodpeckers.

When you can tear yourself away walk forward to the T-junction and turn left with the wood on both sides. To your right is Tatton Park estate. Cross the stream and walk up the incline. Where the road turns sharp right you go left over a stile. It is signposted to Bowdon.

Walk along the wide track at the side of the field to pass a young plantation of long-needled Christmas trees - the sort that are becoming popular because they do not drop their needles. In this plantation these are interspersed with young beech saplings.

The track takes you straight to the M56 and you turn left alongside it. Grass gives way to small stones - hard on the feet but not muddy. When these peter out this path can be exceedingly wet! Turn right over the motorway and follow the signs to Bowdon all the way to its outskirts.

At first the route goes through a very old wood of hazel, oak, silver birch and elderberry. On the ground you might spot lesser celandine and coltsfoot in spring and a carpet of bluebells in May. Cross the stile

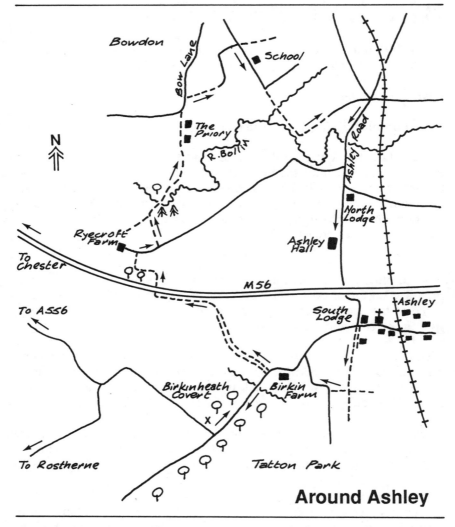

Around Ashley

out of the wood and turn right up the side of a field. Ryecroft Farm is over to your left and you can see the imposing tower of Bowdon Church ahead.

Cross the stile out of the field and turn right along the farm road signposted Ashley Mill and Bowdon. Look out for the broken footpath sign along here and turn left. The noise of the motorway is obtrusive - a pity cars and lorries are not silent! You join another path at the end of this field and veer off to the right.

Scots pines edge the approach to the River Bollin and as you cross this a huge beech tree stands guard over the bridge. Keep straight on to pass a small pond surrounded by a large area of giant hog weed. Be careful not to touch this as it can cause skin problems. Low growing beech and oak, ash and willow, struggle for survival in the wet ground.

Go over the stile out of this area to continue up the field to a further stile. Keep ahead towards Priory Farm with a barbed wire fence on your left. Bear left at the next stile and continue following this fence. The track bears round to the right as you pass the farm and then the Priory itself. Go over two more stiles, climbing stone steps up to the second one, and turn left down the driveway.

You walk through the outskirts of Bowdon on the next part of this walk, with the church high above and the houses clustering up to it. After passing Bowdon Village cricket ground you enter Bow Lane and continue ahead to pass one house and then turn right down a snicket. After passing the cricket pavilion continue down another snicket and along a road, to turn left when you come to Primrose Green building development down Primrose Bank. Turn right past Primrose Cottages and left down Eaton Road to pass by Hamilton Terrace. You finally turn right at the end down York Road and right again to pass Bowdon C. of E. Primary School.

You soon arrive at a signpost to Ashley Mill (Ashley Mill, a 17th century brick building, was damaged by a storm in 1870 and left derelict - there is now nothing left to show where it once was). The route starts off as a tarmac road but soon becomes a path and then a series of stone steps down to the Bollin. Cross the tributary stream gushing under the bridge and keep to the left. The river winds round to meet you and you come to another bridge, this time over the Bollin. At the time of writing, this was under repair and was impassable, so a detour had to be made.

Start this by turning left up the hill and continuing left as you come to the squarely cobbled road called Ashley Mill Lane North. Turn right at the main road and back down the hill which gives you a view of the railway. Cross high over the Bollin using the wooden extension to the old stone bridge, and keep on down Ashley Road until it turns sharp left and you keep ahead into the Tatton Park Estate at North Lodge.

Ashley Hall is an imposing building down here with its stone lintels, Elizabethan chimneys and white walls. The road continues over the motorway where you can spot your earlier route and also see the village of Ashley with its squat church. Pass through the walkers' gate out of the estate as you come to South Lodge.

Cross the main road and go down the grassy track ahead which leads to Ashley Cricket Club. Go over two stiles. I had a chuckle here at the step-ladder stiles out of the cricket field. Are they to speed up the collection of the ball after a six?

Go over the middle of the next field, which is very undulating, and pass between two ponds to make for the stile in the far hedge. Turn right here and right again when you come to a lane. At the main road, which is Lamb Lane, turn left and cross over to walk on the pavement past Birkin Farm. You then retrace your steps back to the car.

AROUND DUNHAM WOODHOUSES

Route: Agden Bridge - River Bollin - Dunham Woodhouses - Bollington - Bridgewater Canal

Distance: 2 to 3 miles

Start: Agden Bridge (SJ 716867)

By Car: Travel on the A50 from Warrington towards Manchester. After passing the 'Dog and Dart' in Grappenhall turn left at the traffic lights onto the A56. After driving through Lymm and travelling towards Altrincham take the first left turn after the traffic lights. Cross over Agden Bridge and park the car here.

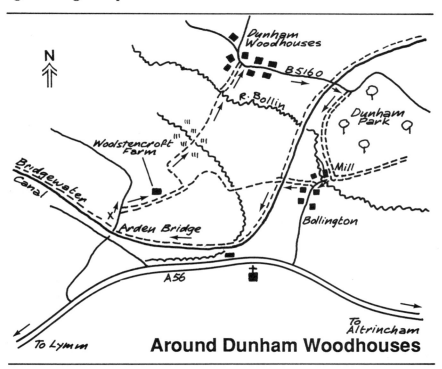

Around Dunham Woodhouses

Walk along the road past Agden Bridge Farm and bear right, crossing a cattle grid into the road marked 'Private, Woolstencroft Farm'. In front of the farm bear right again. Continue gingerly along a very mucky track past the farm.

When you reach a stile do not cross over it but go through the gate on your left. Walk round two sides of this field keeping the hedge on your left. You may have to negotiate your way through a herd of Friesians on the way. Be intrepid! They are big but harmless! Climb over the stile in the far corner of the field.

You will see another stile in front of you. Cross the rough ground to it, and use the stout, conveniently-placed plank to cross the deep ditch on the way. The right of way now goes straight across the field in front of you, and there should be a signpost in the middle of the field indicating this. At the far side climb over the fence with care. Drop down to the stream and go across the sturdy bridge.

Cross this field until you arrive at the River Bollin and a gate. This pleasant little river rises in moorland near Macclesfield, and ends up as one of the chief feeder rivers of the Mersey and the Manchester Ship Canal. Go through the gate and bear left over the river onto a muddy track which becomes Meadow Lane, and leads you into Dunham Woodhouses. The woodsmen working on the Dunham Massey estate used to occupy the cottages in this tiny hamlet.

When you come to the road turn right. You will soon go under the Bridgewater Canal. It isn't difficult to imagine the early barges loaded with cargo being pulled along by a plodding horse. When you reach a private road just before a bus stop turn right. You are now skirting the boundary of Dunham Park.

At the end of this road you will come to an old flour mill. Its huge wheel used to be turned by water diverted from the Bollin. Until recently it was used to store fertilizer, but soon it will be developed into luxury flats. Take the right fork here and cross the millrace by a narrow footbridge. Walk into the village of Bollington, past 'The Swan With Two Nicks'. Its name refers to the practice of putting nicks into the beak of a swan to establish ownership. Dick Turpin is reputed to have called here regularly on his journeys north.

Swan with Two Nicks, Bollington.

Turn right at the small village green dominated by its oak tree, and follow the cobbled track under the canal. A friendly donkey may greet you with its loud braying on the way! On the far side of the canal go through the gap in the low wall and climb up the bank onto the tow path. When the canal was a busy waterway a passenger boat called 'The Packet' stopped at the wharf here at 9 a.m. each morning to take people to Manchester. Its shrill whistle heralded its arrival.

Turn right along the towpath. You will see the small church built in Gothic style, and will then pass 'Ye Olde No. Three' which is reputed to have three ghosts - all of them friendly! It got its name from being the third stop for a change of horses for the 'Chester Fliers', the fast passenger boats which plied between Chester and Manchester in the 19th century (the name 'Chester Flier' is now the local nickname for the express diesel trains operating between Chester and Manchester). You go under Agden Bridge and reach the end of your walk.

AROUND HIGH LEGH

Route: Pheasant Walk - Wrenshot Lane - Peacock Lane - West Lane - The Avenue

Distance: 2 to 3 miles

Start: B5159 in High Legh (SJ 699841)

By Car: Take the A50 south from Warrington and stay on it until you turn left along the B5159 signposted to Partington and Carrington. Park on a straight stretch of road along here, between Pheasant Walk and the sign to St. John's Church.

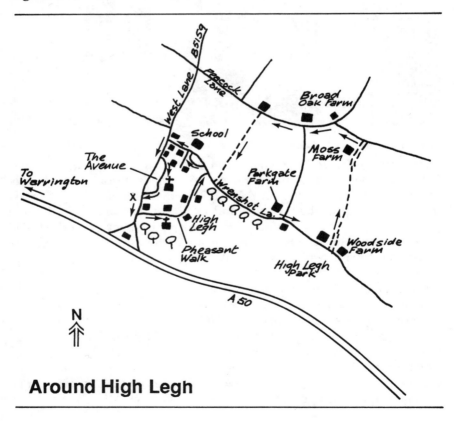

Around High Legh

Walk back and turn left down Pheasant Walk. There used to be two estates at High Legh, and a high brick wall was all that separated them. Part of this can still be seen as you walk down here. The halls have now been demolished but the private chapels still remain. St. Mary's is the first one you come to. It was built in 1586 and is one of the oldest buildings in the area. It is unused now but is in an attractive setting completely surrounded by a well-maintained lawn, and shaded by yew trees and other bushes.

Continue down the hill. Robert Moffatt is remembered with pride here. He started work as the gardener's boy on the estate but left his native land to become a famous missionary in Africa. Turn right onto Wrenshot Lane, where you walk alongside a private wood. Pass Parkgate Farm, ignoring the road that comes in on the left here, and continue past a thatched cottage that is beautifully renovated. All the outbuildings and barns are thatched in the same pattern, which makes a delightful whole.

Turn left at Woodside Farm. After passing the farmhouse there is a small white gate next to the main gate and you go through this into the farmyard, then out of the other side, bearing left along the track. When this ends, go through the right-hand gate and continue down the field keeping the hedge on your left. Carry on through the gate into the next field, still 'hugging' the hedge of thick hawthorn. Make sure that you shut all the gates and fasten them securely.

Go over the narrow stile at the end of this field - all the stiles on this part of the walk tend to be a tight squeeze! Continue on down the side of the next field. Take care to keep as near to the hedge as you can without getting prickled, especially when there are crops growing. Continue over two more stiles, through the gate into the farmyard of Moss Farm, over another stile, and along the road past the farmhouse turning left along Peacock Lane.

Continue past Broad Oak Farm, enjoying the sweeping views over grassy fields. When you come to the next house, with its old-fashioned lamp and its birdhouse in the garden, turn left down the tractor track which runs down the side of the field. From the wide stile at the end of this field the footpath is a definite line ahead and the modern buildings of High Legh Primary School come into view. Go through the kissing gate and cross the next field, keeping the telegraph poles on your right aa you make for the corner of the garden opposite. When you cross the stile you are back onto Wrenshot Lane. There is a convenient stone here to wipe the mud off your boots!

Turn right and you can soon bear left through a little 'park' which brings you back onto the road a little way along. Keep on this road until you turn left into West Lane. Pass the stocks, dated 1843 but probably older than that. Then turn left up the Avenue, past St. John's Church with its black and white front, red roofs and sandstone base. There are several large boulders in front of it, each weighing several tons. They are thought to have been deposited by a glacier at the end of the Ice Age. You soon reach West Lane again and the end of your walk.

Ancient Stocks at High Legh.

AROUND LYMM

Route: Crouchley Lane - Granthams - A50 - Broadheys Lane - Lymm Dam

Distance: 2 to 3 miles

Start: Behind the church in Crouchley Lane (SJ 684867)

By Car: Take the A50 from Warrington. After passing 'The Dog and Dart' in Grappenhall turn left onto the A56 to Lymm. After passing Lymm Dam and St. Mary's Church turn right into Crouchley Lane. There is plenty of parking space here.

The first part of this walk continues down Crouchley Lane. This is a pleasant country road which has wide open views over the surrounding countryside. The unmistakably English sound of church bells may accompany you on your way. You soon pass Yew Tree Farm which delivers milk provided by its Friesian herd of cows. After rounding a corner turn right, dropping down to cross Mag Brook in its tiny valley. This is one of the streams that feeds Lymm Dam.

Cross the stile just after the private road goes off to Granthams, and just before the road you have been walking along rises over the motorway. Make for the corner of the cottage garden and then cross the field down to the stream. Climb over the two 'stepladder' stiles here and go straight across the field ahead.

There is a stile at the right-hand corner of the wood which takes you along a path through the wood and over another stile out of it. Then keep the wood on your right until, at the end of it, you work your way past the pools, immersed in a still silence of their own, and continue along the hedge to the motorway.

Cross the stile beside the iron gate painted red. This seems to be a feature of the farm here. Go along this disused roadway until you turn right onto the A50 for a short way. In the distance you will have a glimpse of the pinnacled tower of St Mary's church, with its

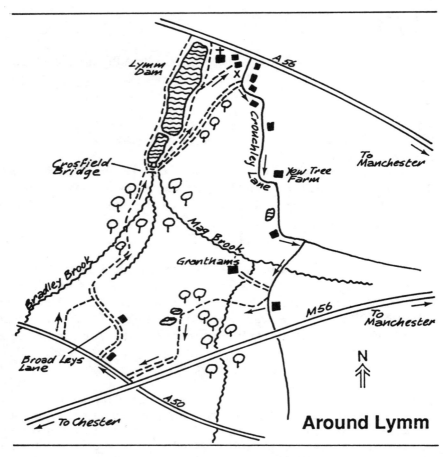

Around Lymm

surrounding poplars. These tall, pointed trees, clearly visible on the skyline, were planted by Lord Leverhulme.

Pass Broadheys Lane and Primrose Hill Nurseries. Then turn right over the stile at the signpost. Keep alongside the hedge here, bearing right to another stile. Turn left along the track until it ends at a field. Climb the stile, with the burbling stream beside you as it drops out of a pipe, and carry on beside it to the wood and another stile.

Turn left and then right along the path through the wood. The undergrowth in this part is still a tangled mass of rhododendrons and brambles. When you reach Bradley Brook cross the substantial stepping stones and turn right, staying in the wood. You will notice how the rangers have cleared and tidied this area. Carry on along this path until it climbs up to Crosfield Bridge. This imposing structure was built in 1918 by Lord Leverhulme. He had plans for a housing development in the area, but these were never carried out.

Walk over this bridge and follow the lakeside footpath back to your car. Lymm Dam was formed early in the 19th century at a time when new industry was developing in the area and the village needed more water to power new machinery. Nowadays it is a notable beauty spot. The great crested grebe breed on it and fishermen along the bank hope for a worthwhile catch of carp or pike.

AROUND MILLINGTON

Route: Hope Cottage - M56 - Booth Bank - Millington Hall

Distance: 2 to 3 miles

Start: Millington Lane (SJ 730845)

By Car: Travel on the A50 from Warrington and turn left at Mere traffic lights. Go straight through the traffic lights at Bucklow Hill and then take the second left down Millington Lane. You can park where the road goes off to Millington Hall on the left.

Around Millington

52

The footpath is signed opposite at the side of a house. As you walk down it, enjoy the magnificent views right over to the foothills of the Pennines, with Bowdon Church forming a nearer landmark. The murmur of the traffic on the fast-moving roadways is not obtrusive. The very straightness of the Chester to Manchester road suggests its Roman origin, as it follows the line of the ancient Watling Street.

Go over the stile and straight across the next field to the far corner towards the intersection of motorways. You cross the stile and go through the gate on the left. Make for the cottage over to the left across this field. There is a stile at the corner of the garden and then another one which brings you onto a farm track. Pass the peace of Hope Cottage on your left with its thick holly hedge surround, and continue along the grassy track.

Do not cross the motorway here but turn left alongside it down the side of the field. At the far hedge turn away from the motorway, and if you are short you might find it easier to go under the stile in the hedge rather than over it. Go along the side of the next field parallel with the wood. Your presence may persuade a brace of partridges to leave the hedge in a flurry of annoyance. Carry on ahead at the stile into the next field, leaving the wood behind. Halfway along this field turn right through the large gap in the hedge and carry on down the track to Booth Bank Farm and Reddy Lane.

Turn immediately left and you will see the footpath sign into the field over to the right. There is a good parking spot here for those wishing to do the walk a different way round. Keep along the side of the hill parallel to the stream. The friendly horses may follow you along, hoping for titbits. Cross the stile at the end of the field and bear over to the right to cross the stream. You then keep beside it all the way to a farm track where you re-cross it and puff your way up the hill to the farm.

At the top turn away from the large barn on your right and negotiate the rusty gate. Go left along the side of the field for a very short distance, and, if you have sharp eyes, you will see a narrow way up through the crops. The stile ahead comes into view as you breast the hill. Turn right along the road and back to your car.

AROUND OUGHTRINGTON

Route: Pepper Street - Oughtrington Lane - Bridgewater Canal - Burford Lane - St. Peter's Church - Longbutt Lane - Church Green - The Dingle - Lymm Cross

Distance: 2 to 3 miles

Start: The car park off Pepper Street (SJ 684872)

By Car: Take the A50 from Warrington. After passing 'The Dog and Dart' in Grappenhall turn left at the traffic lights onto the A56. On reaching Lymm turn left onto the A6144. When you get to Lymm Cross in the centre of the village turn into Pepper Street and park in the car-park there.

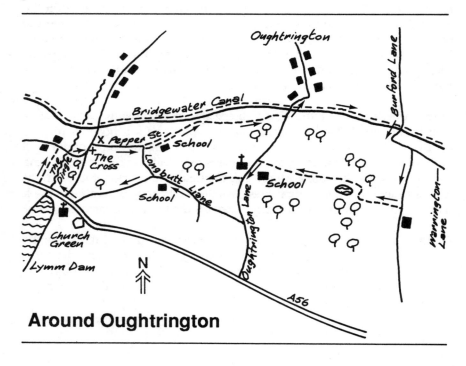

Around Oughtrington

Walk along Pepper Street away from the village. The first part of the road is cobbled and is thought to date from Roman times. After passing Ravenbank Primary School carry on down the footpath, making sure you don't turn right up to the caravan storage park. The angular shape of Oughtrington parish church soon comes into view. It is a dominant landmark on much of this walk.

When you reach Oughtrington Lane turn left over Lloyd Bridge - referred to by the locals as Dog Bridge. Drop down onto the towpath and turn left along it. You next go under Grantham's Bridge which takes a farm track over the canal. At the far side of Burford Lane underbridge go down the steps off the towpath. This exit is interesting as there are steps for people and a slope where horses could be taken down in earlier times. Go under the canal here and along Burford Lane. Ignore Warrington Lane coming in from your left and continue up the hill until you see a footpath sign to the right.

Follow the footpath signs into the wood and out along the field at the other side. You have a glimpse of Lymm High School here which is partly Elizabethan. When you reach the road turn left and pass St Peter's parish church before turning right along another footpath. This church was built in 1874 by a local cotton manufacturer. All the woodwork inside is of oak, except the pews which are made of deal. 'Cotton' hit a bad patch when the wood for these was due to be ordered! Along here you have a very good view of the Thelwall viaduct which takes the M6 over the Manchester Ship Canal. All the Cheshire part of the M6 was finally completed in 1963.

Turn right along Longbutt Lane which possibly formed the original boundary between Lymm and Oughtrington. After passing the school carry on along the path keeping the football pitches on your right. When you come to a road turn right even though it is a cul-de-sac. There is a cut through at the end which will quickly bring you to 'Church Green'. Carry on past the church down Church Road, and as you pass Lymm Dam turn right down some steps. This is referred to locally as 'The Dingle'. It is a gorge with walls 100 feet high.

When you reach the weir look up the road to your left and you will see 'The Spread Eagle' with the large brass bird that forms the inn sign. Lymm is well-endowed with inns (there are five in the village itself and

Lymm Cross.

a number on the outskirts). The settlement has actually been built on a rock, and around here you can see how the streets and houses have been cut out of the rock face.

You then turn right to Lymm Cross. This is one of the best examples of a village cross still in existence. It stands on a weathered flight of sandstone steps and rumour has it that St. Paul preached from them. Certainly, it used to act as a rostrum for both preachers and speakers. Above the steps each sundial has a different inscription on it and the village stocks stand nearby.

Cock fighting also used to take place in the square and Lymm may have been the last place in England for this cruel pastime to be abolished. An old Cheshire rhyme refers to the colours of the game cocks bred in this area for the sport.

'Lymon Greys,
Statham Blacks,
Warburton Blue
And Peover Pecks.' (speckled)

You may wish to spend more time in this pretty village before walking up from the Cross back to the car-park.

AROUND ROSTHERNE

Route: Rostherne - Tatton Dale - Mere Farm - Bucklow Hill - Rostherne
Church

Distance: 2 to 3 miles

Start: Rostherne village (SJ 743836)

By Car: Take the A50 from Warrington and when you come to the
traffic lights at Mere turn left towards Manchester. Turn right at the next
set of lights and immediately left to Rostherne. You should be able to
park at the side of the road in the village.

Walk back out of the village towards Bucklow Hill and turn left down
the first track you come to, which is at the end of the first field and leads
into it. Keep down the side of this field and go through the kissing gate
which is in the far corner. Make for the far corner of the wood over to
your left. Cross over into the next field here and there is a clear path
ahead to Home Farm at Tatton Dale.

Turn right at the road and walk down past the farm. Just after you pass
the old cottage dated 1626 turn right into the field, passing the old barn
at the back of the cottage. The path across the field is well defined again.
Go over, or under the fence you come to, depending on your size! Carry
straight on towards Mere Farm. It is aptly named. The two meres look
very pretty fringed by reeds and encircled by trees. Cross over the
stream and follow the 'rabbit track' over the next field, keeping Mere
Farm to your left.

Go through the gate onto the farm road and turn right along this pretty
little valley, which has a very attractive waterfall cascading down into it.
The footpath leads off to the left before the depot. You go over the stile
and across the stream. Climb up out of the valley and cross the planks
beside the gate into the next field.

Follow the orange bands on the posts that lead over this field. You cross
the stile into the next field and drop down to the mere. There are even
stepping stones over the marshy ground. This idyllic spot is the fishing

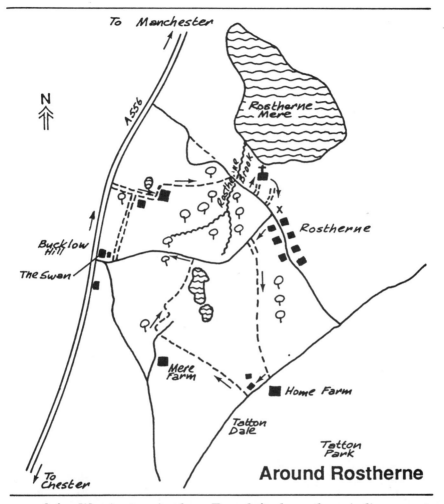

To Manchester

N

A 556

Rostherne Mere

Rostherne Brook

Rostherne

Bucklow Hill

The Swan

Mere Farm

Home Farm

Tatton Dale

Tatton Park

Around Rostherne

To Chester

ground for Warrington Anglers. Turn left along the winding country lane towards Bucklow Hill.

Just before you reach the first building (part of the Old Swan Hotel) turn right down a farm track. Pass Denfield Hall Farm and turn right along the A556 to the next turn which goes to Denfield Farm. Walk past the duckpond then go left through a gate. Rostherne Church is an outstanding landmark in the distance. Carry on down the side of the field and through the kissing gate at the end of it. A rabbit track continues straight across the field ahead and Rostherne Mere comes into view.

This is the largest natural lake in Cheshire and is over 100 feet deep in places. It is maintained as a national nature reserve and bird sanctuary, and smelt, a small, salt-water fish which spawns in rivers like salmon, is one of the species to be found in it.

Go through the narrow opening at the end of the field and drop down through the wood turning right along the road. You cross Rostherne Brook along here as it gushes rapidly out of the wood and over the meadowland to the mere. If you are doing this walk on Easter Sunday, listen for the mermaid which local legend says has made her home in the mere. The only evidence of her occupancy, is supposed to occur on Easter Sunday when she can be heard singing, and ringing a bell she has found on the bed of the lake.

Turn left through the lychgate to St. Mary's Church. This entrance into

Rostherne Church.

the churchyard dates from 1640 and is probably the oldest gate in Cheshire. It closes automatically by a weighted cord passing round a wheel above it. The dominant church tower houses six bells and there is an old Cheshire rhyme which says,

'Higher Peover kettles,
Lower Peover pans,
Knutsford sweet roses
And Rostherne great drones.'

It is well worthwhile taking a detour round the back of the church to admire the view before you carry on up through the churchyard and out of the top gate to end your walk.

AROUND NORTHWICH

Antrobus
Arley
Davenham
Great Budworth
Little Leigh
Lower Whitley
Plumley

The Pathfinder map that you need for these walks is Northwich and Knutsford - Sheet SJ67/77. Travelling instructions are given from Northwich. Great Budworth is the longest walk, being about six miles. Little Leigh is five and Davenham is four. The walks around Antrobus, Arley, Lower Whitley and Plumley are all two to three miles long and will take between one and two hours to complete.

For visitors to the area, the walks around Arley and Antrobus would combine well with a visit to the house and gardens of Arley Hall, which are open to the public, except during the winter months. One of the attractions is a tithe barn, where the tenants on the estate once came to pay their money (a tenth of their income) to the Lord of the Manor. This is an excellent example of a cruck-framed building.

The Great Budworth walk circles around the outside of Marbury Park, an area of parkland surrounded by woods. It offers several walks of its own, whilst naturalists and bird watchers would particularly enjoy the wildlife around the mere. For man-made entertainment, Pickmere offers a variety of boats for hire and also has a funfair.

The Salt Museum in Northwich gives an interesting insight into the industry responsible for the development of the town. The building that houses the exhibition used to be the workhouse for the area. It is open all the year round on every afternoon except Monday

AROUND ANTROBUS

Route: Park Farm - Whitley Reed Cottage - Stretton Airfield - Pennypleck House

Distance: 2 to 3 miles

Start: Sandilands Farm (SJ 661826)

By Car: Take the A49 from Warrington and turn left at Stretton traffic lights. Turn right at the church in Appleton Thorn. You will soon reach a straight stretch of road known locally as the Arley Mile. When you get to a crossroads with a grassy triangle turn sharp left. Carry on along here, ignoring a road coming in on the right, until you eventually reach Sandilands Farm. Here there is a wide area at the side of the road where you can park.

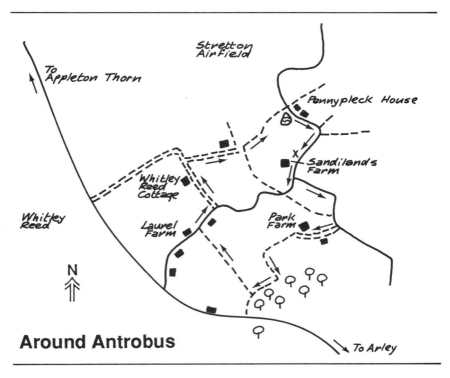

Around Antrobus

Walk back along the road you have travelled in the car. Turn left at the first footpath sign and climb over the high stile into the field. (It is preferable to avoid sitting on the barbed wire fencing at the side of the stile!) The line of the path ahead is well marked by leaves and brown earth. Climb the difficult stile out of the field and immediately turn right to Park Farm and Crowley Green Cottage. The dogs will herald your arrival along here. Many years ago the postman used to travel around these parts in a horse-drawn red van. He would blow a whistle at the farm gates for people to come and collect their mail.

Go through the farmyard and continue along a cart-track which soon becomes a wide, grassy ride. At the very end of this go through the right-hand gate and walk down the edge of the field to the wood. Listen for the burbling of the underground brook as it briefly surfaces in a small area of low, rough ground along here.

Turn right at the dark wood. The name 'Antrobus' actually means 'amid woods'. Continue along the side of this one crossing two stiles. The second stile takes you briefly into the wood, and another one takes you

The Well at Pennypleck House.

straight out of it and up the side of the field. The white walls of Laurel Farm soon come into view. After climbing two more stiles you are back on the road.

Turn right along the road and then left down a private road which passes Whitley Reed Cottage. Over to the left is an area known as Whitley Reed. This used to be one of the deepest and wildest areas of marshland in Cheshire. Now the only trace of it is to be found in the names of the farms and woods in the area.

Where this road forks bear right. The grassy banks and disused buildings of Stretton Airfield are clearly visible over to the left. This airfield was much in use during the last war. Nowadays the neglected runways are only used by local youngsters learning to drive.

As you pass the farm notice the sign 'P.E.W. 1905' over the door. It is probably the initials of the builder and the year that the house was built. The cart-track ends here but keep ahead, with the hedge beside you. After the stile at the end of the field you walk beside the steep banks of a small beck and end up at a small pond.

Turn right to pass Pennypleck House. You might wonder what cricket enthusiast devised the unusual wind vane. The water butts look as if they serve a useful purpose, strategically positioned to catch the rainwater. There is also a wishing-well in the garden. Carry on along this road and back to your car.

AROUND ARLEY

Route: Arley - M6 - Hobbs Hill Lane - The Ashes - Arley Green

Distance: 2 to 3 miles

Start: The small car-park in Arley village (SJ 670809)

By Car: Take the A49 from Warrington and turn left at Stretton traffic lights. Turn right at Appleton Thorn church. Continue down this road to Arley. Park your car in the grassy car-park on the left as you come into the small hamlet.

Walk on down the road towards Arley Hall. The original Lord of the Manor at Arley made up hunting songs and other rhymes, and several of the latter still exist on the signposts bordering the estate. The first one you see is very weathered with age but you can just make out the words,

> 'Trespassers this notice heed
> Onward you may not proceed
> Unless to Arley Hall you speed.'

Proceed through this gate anyway! Then turn left at the next old sign. The fields bordering the estate here may be full of sheep, so if you have a dog accompanying you keep it under strict control.

After rounding the bend, follow the sign to High Legh, which is dedicated to the Founder of Altrincham Rambling Club. When the road turns left over the stream you keep straight on beside it until you cross it half-way down the next field. Keep near the stream until you have crossed another stile. When the stream veers away to the right leave it and follow the line of telegraph poles to the bridge over the M6. In the middle of this field you pass a tree stump covered with several varieties of fungi.

Cross the motorway and when the road forks keep to the right. You may see rabbits in the spinney here. On reaching the end of Hobbs Hill Lane turn right and keep straight ahead as you pass Northwood Cottage.

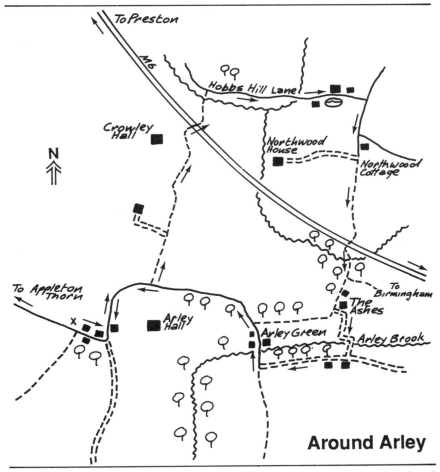

Around Arley

When the road goes right to Northwood House you go straight ahead again through the white posts and the side gate. This is weighted to make sure it falls shut behind you, but make doubly sure by fastening the 'chain and peg' as well.

Carry on down the side of the field, making for the motorway bridge, which you cross and carry on over a stream flowing in a very deep trench. The hens at the farm will complain loudly at your intrusion. They are an attractive variety, with sleek black feathers, red coxcombs and yellow colouring around their eyes.

Go left around the side of 'The Ashes', a very old house dating from the 16th century. Turn right immediately to cross Arley Brook, and then right again at a row of old cottages, one of which was an old lodge on the estate. Notice the towering beech trees with their smooth grey trunks as you walk down here.

Turn right into Arley Green, a model estate village built in the Tudor-style in the mid-19th century by the lord of the manor, Rowland Egerton-Warburton. He even revived Maypole Dancing on the purpose-built green. The cobbled road ahead was the original drive to the Hall and you get a good side view of the building along here. It is not the original hall but was built in the 1830s in Jacobean style. The gardens are also well worth a visit. One of the first herbaceous borders in the country was planted here. Carry on along this road back to the car.

AROUND DAVENHAM

Route: River Dane - Gad Brook - Trent and Mersey Canal - Shipbrook Hill

Distance: 4 miles

Start: A lay-by on Church Street near the River Dane (SJ 871711)

By Car: Take the A533 south from Northwich. Keep straight on at the Northwich by-pass (A556) roundabout. In the centre of the village of Davenham turn left down Church Street to pass the church and the rectory. Before crossing the River Dane there is a lay-by on your right where you can park.

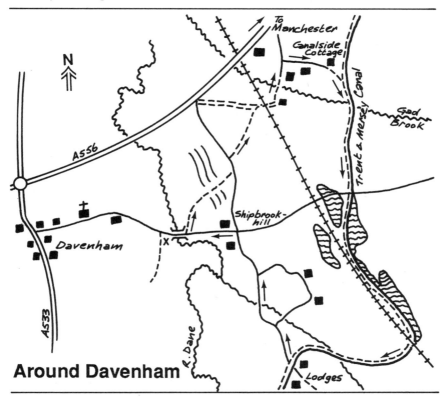

Around Davenham

The first part of this walk is the most difficult as, at the time of writing, there was no well-defined path between crops, but it is worth persevering for the interesting terrain and delightful views as you breast the hilltop.

The stiles in this part of central Cheshire are a little different from normal too. They can be plainly seen in most of the hawthorn hedges as they are stout wooden structures of three bars joined to two uprights but there is no piece across the bottom bar to give you a leg up!

As you start the walk you can see the modern buildings of Leftwich High School rising out of a housing estate, while in the nearer distance tall poplars march along. Behind you the Victorian outline of Davenham church points to the sky. Its spire was originally built in 1850 and after recent renovation is now complete again.

Walk ahead across the stone bridge over the River Dane, one of several tributaries of the Mersey, and turn immediately left over the fence into a field. From here, if you look to the top of the slope ahead you can see the stile in the hedge up there. You are making for this.

To reach it, first make for the corner of the hedge opposite you and continue down this hedge but a little way from it. There should be a stile in the facing hedge at the bottom of the steeply sloping ground. I found the remains of it but had to scramble through the gap near it.

Climb straight up the hill to the stile in the hedge at the top - which is the one you could see at the start of the walk. You have to negotiate this stile and cope with the thick and prickly hawthorn hedge at the same time. Continue straight across the field to the next stile in the hedge ahead. Cross this and turn left for a very short way along the road. The rest of the walk is plain sailing!

When you come to two gates on your right there is a stile between them. Climb over or under this and go down the side of the field with the hedge on your right. The bridge over the railway comes into view ahead, and when you reach the stile at the end of the field you turn right onto the track that takes you over the railway.

Turn left off this track just before the farm and cut down to the brook where it goes under the ground here. Make your way alongside it until you cross Gad Brook and go over an iron stile and up a footpath which becomes a lane. Roberts' bakery and some modern factories are visible over to your left. After passing Elke's Biscuit Factory continue until you reach Canalside Cottage where you bear right through a gate and along a short path which brings you to a stile onto the canal towpath. This is the Trent-and-Mersey Canal, built to join the industrial Midlands to the port of Liverpool.

Turn right to pass boats lined up on the opposite bank contrasting with fishermen on the towpath side. The noise of the Northwich bypass in the distance is the only distraction to an otherwise peaceful part of the walk, perhaps with the sun shimmering on the water as an added bonus.

Go under bridge number 181. There are several relics of the canal from when it used to be a busy waterway along here - milestones, beams under a corrugated iron roof, a wooden colliery boat at what must have once been a busy wharf. You may see Hercules, a large iron barge manned by two men employed to tidy the hedgerows and burn the wood.

There are several areas where the original bank has disappeared completely and large areas of lake have formed. Isolated posts are left to show the original line of the bank. These places have become reed-fringed meres - a birds' paradise. Listen for curlews calling too.

The railway moves towards the canal here and then runs parallel to it for quite a way. You cross a causeway before walking under the iron bridge supported by brick pillars which takes the railway over the canal. As you walk away from the railway a country road runs alongside the canal and you pass the derelict remains of a bridge.

A tributary of the Dane flows under the canal and the scolding of chaffinches may herald your arrival at a little coppice of beeches and ash trees. The spire of Davenham Church appears again and you may hear a woodpecker jabbing its beak into a tree. As you come to the Lodges and bridge number 179 look out for the lifelike heron standing motionless in the garden. I was completely fooled until I saw the same model in a garden elsewhere.

71

Leave the towpath here, climbing some sandstone steps and turning right along the road. Keep straight on, ignoring two turns to the right. You cross the stream again as it ripples through a wood. When you reach the crossroads turn left and cross over the River Dane to return to your car.

Canal Mile Post.

AROUND GREAT BUDWORTH

Route: Budworth Mere - Anderton - Trent and Mersey Canal - Marston - Higher Marston

Distance: 6 miles

Start: Near Brownslow House (SJ 656774)

By Car: Take the A559 north from Northwich. After passing through Marston and rounding a badly cambered bend take the next turn left. Park into the side of the road just before Brownslow House where the road is straight and wide.

This is a walk with much of interest to see. Outstanding landmarks are never far out of sight, for instance, the crenellated tower of Great Budworth Church, and the vastness of the ICI Mond Division Works at Winnington. When the skyline is filled by the mass of this industry it is easy to see how Northwich became known as 'the Black Country of the North'. Dr. Ludwig Mond founded ICI and his statue stands amid the huge chemical works lining the river.

Although parts of the route can be muddy, it passes near so many different kinds of water such as meres, flashes and canals, it is well worth putting up with the occasional slosh!

After parking the car, walk ahead past Brownslow House and Brownslow Cottages before turning left into the wood at the footpath sign. Drop down through the wood. Towering beeches stand sentinel on either side of the path. You emerge from the other side to cross the field ahead and Budworth Mere comes into view. It was used as a fish hatchery in the Middle Ages and even now is well stocked with bream and pike. Reed warblers and great crested grebes breed in its reeds. Marbury Country Park borders its southern shore and is well worth a visit for bird watching or other natural pursuits!

You eventually join the fence on your right, keeping alongside it to

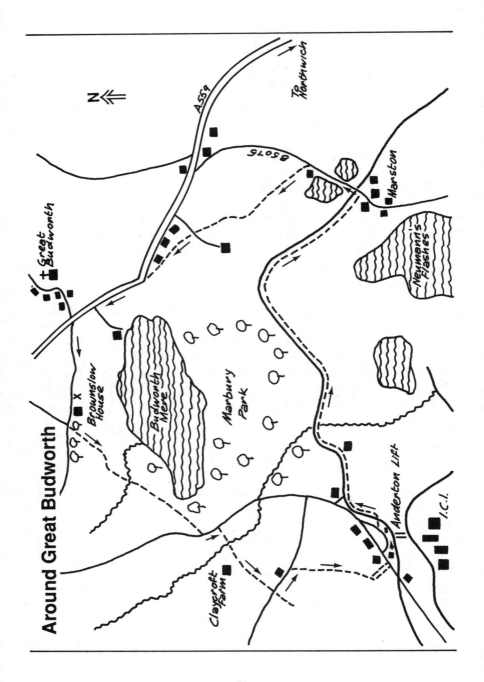

Around Great Budworth

Anderton Boat Lift.

avoid the lower ground which tends to be boggy. Continue forward over the stream. There is a wide bridge for cows and farm vehicles and a footbridge with a handrail for walkers. Keep forward with the barbed wire fence on your right. Cross the stile and carry on across the next field to the little wooden gate in the hedge ahead. This will bring you out onto the road.

Turn left and immediately right down a footpath to Anderton. Keep the hawthorn hedge on your right and go forward, crossing the stile into the wood and then going over a well-made bridge with ornate railings. After crossing a further stile out of the wood, keep forward across the field to the stile at the side of the gate ahead. Claycroft Farm is to your right and the path across the next field is very clearly defined. Turn left when you reach the road and the industrial landscape of ICI comes into prominent view.

When you reach the house on your left turn right where the footpath sign indicates. Cross straight over this field to the stile in the hedge opposite and keep ahead with the field boundary to your right. Cross the next stile and make for a further stile in the facing barbed wire fence.

This is slightly over to your left. The final stile is across the next field in the left-hand corner of the hedge.

Follow the track down to turn left at the road and into the village of Anderton. There is a well-stocked village shop a few yards along here where you can buy snacks. If you are not making this detour, turn right down Old Road to the Anderton Boat Lift, passing the large local coach firm of Walkers and the Stanley Arms pub.

The Anderton Boat Lift is one of the wonders of Cheshire. This incredible construction was the first of its kind in the world and is the only remaining one in Britain. Its purpose is to raise and lower boats 50 feet 4 inches between the Trent-and-Mersey Canal and the River Weaver. Using a system of locks this used to take one-and-a-half hours but the lift replaced these and took five minutes. It was first opened in 1875 and was operated by a hydraulic mechanism. This was converted to an electric operation in 1907. The lift was closed by the British Water Board in August 1983, due to the corrosion of the main support legs. There have been many protests about its prolonged closure and work is currently underway to repair it.

Cross the footbridge over the canal and turn left to walk along the towpath. There is a sheltered picnic spot that drops down off the bank here and gives a good view of the lift and the cranes repairing it. You have a close-up view of ICI too.

Continue along the towpath, walking under rectangular bridges and past old iron signposts indicating the mileage from Preston Brook and Shardlow. Boats are moored along the opposite bank and you shortly come to Anderton Marina with its large variety of brightly-coloured longboats for hire. Cross the bridge that goes over the cut to Clare Cruisers and continue along the towpath. You soon pass the cottage called Jackson's Turn. Notice the sturdy iron rings set in the concrete, where boats can be moored.

The canal forms the southern boundary of Marbury Park along here and one gets a glimpse of the parkland through the trees. You may be lucky enough to spot a red squirrel scampering around. And don't miss the mighty beech tree, its branches spread wide, its trunk algae-covered and pockmarked.

Ahead is the modern village of Marston, its houses looking from a distance as if they have been made out of plasticene. Budworth Church, made of local stone, is a prominent landmark too. It has been described as, 'a church that sits on a knoll with cottages clustered around it like a hen with her chicks'. You pass another iron signpost - black and white like a panda. This is a stretch of the canal to stride along in the nipping wind.

A brightly coloured sign advertises The Salt Barge - an apt name for the 'local'. The derelict buildings of the Lion Salt Works are ahead. It was the only place still to be producing salt by the 'open pan' method, until it went bankrupt a few years ago. It serves as a reminder that the prosperity of Northwich has always been based on salt. In fact the area still accounts for two-thirds of the rock salt produced in this country for use on roads in winter. Neuman's Flashes over to your right is the largest of the salt lakes (flashes are the result of the sudsidence of old salt workings). You also catch a glimpse of Witton Church here It is the oldest building in Northwich and its roof originally came from Norton Priory.

When you reach the bridge climb up off the towpath and turn left onto the B5075 pausing on the bridge to look at the village. This area is built on pillars of salt that are slowly dissolving. Whole houses have been lost, tumbling without warning into the old brine pits. Notice the switchback streets with buildings that look ready to topple.

Continue along the road between two smaller flashes, also the result of subsidence caused by pumping out the brine from beneath the surface. Bullrushes fringe the banks and these wild areas are the haunts of swans, ducks, coots and anglers.

Just past Harris's there is a footpath sign to the left. Bright yellow arrows clearly define the way along the sides of the fields. Marston Hall is nearby and you get a final glimpse of the Trent-and-Mersey Canal as it comes out of Marbury Woods where you have just walked. Follow the barbed wire fence across the field towards Great Budworth church and revel in this rare bit of Tudor England. The rumble of traffic on the road ahead will bring you back to the present day.

You come to a step-ladder stile, perhaps amidst a sea of mud, which

Great Budworth Pumphouse.

leads you to another clearly indicated stile and with luck you will be able to step out of the ooze without sitting in it! Go down the field, keeping the barbed wire fence on your left. You are heading for the backs of the houses that run parallel with the road ahead. A small herd of cows huddled together for warmth, their backs to the wind, the last time I was here.

Cross the stile, the lane, and another stile signposted to Great Budworth, and keep along behind the houses. Drop down to the A road where it turns a sharp bend, crossing to the safety of the footpath.

Great Budworth Church is visible in great detail here. The village was much restored and rebuilt in the 19th century by Rowland Egerton-Warburton of Arley (Great Budworth was then part of the Arley estate). It was once the centre of the largest parish in Cheshire, covering 35 townships. You pass the more recent innovation of Great Budworth Sailing Club. Boats with their tall masts cluster at haphazard angles around the clubhouse.

Just before you turn left at the crossroads there is an interesting pump and pumphouse. This was the source of drinking water for Great Budworth village until 1934. It is worth turning aside to read the interesting rhyme thanking God for the underground spring that pours out of the ground here.

The walk back to the car is lightened by a lovely view of the full extent of Budworth Mere, the chimneys and buildings of ICI providing a contrasting backdrop.

AROUND LITTLE LEIGH

Route: Little Leigh - Trent and Mersey Canal - Saltersford Tunnel - Barnton - Stone Heyes Lane - Deslay Heath Farm - Blue Grass Animal Hotel

Distance: 5 miles

Start: Near Woodward's Abattoir (SJ 618772)

By Car: Take the A49 from Warrington and turn left at the Little Chef onto the A533 towards Barnton and Northwich. Take the first turn left and, after passing Ash Tree Farm, park beside the road just before the entrance to the Blue Grass Animal Hotel.

Walk forward and follow the public footpath (sometimes hidden by a laburnum tree) which appears to go through the garden of a house. There is a stile at the back of the garden, a short path and then another stile into the field ahead. This takes a bit of negotiating!

Keep the hedge on your right and continue to another stile, then down the field to the stream. Go through the gate and up the next field, making for a left-hand corner halfway across it where there is a stile. Cross this into another field, where you keep the hedge again on your right until you reach a stile onto the A533.

Cross the busy road and go down the footpath opposite keeping the hawthorn hedge on your right. The slim spire of Little Leigh church becomes visible briefly. This is St. Michael's and its walls are said to be of a hot orange colour. Carry on up the next field to the stile ahead. When I did this walk there were several horses here, munching hay in the winter sunlight. Cross the white stile into the next field and walk diagonally across it to the stile in the left-hand corner of the facing hedge.

Turn right along the country lane called Leigh Lane and almost immediately left down a wide cart track that winds between hedges of hawthorn, ash and bramble, a lane typical of Cheshire. The main track ends at a field but you keep forward towards a small wood. There are

Around Little Leigh

wide views here and more horses. You can hear the little stream gurgling busily down through the wood. The path beside the wood may be quite muddy, so take care.

When you reach a lane turn left along it to cross a bridge and drop down through a gap in the fence onto the towpath of the Trent-and-Mersey Canal. Turn right along the towpath towards Barnton. Nearby you can see the swing bridge over the River Weaver at Acton Bridge. The two waterways run very close together here. You come to an attractive arched bridge in the middle of absolutely nowhere and then pass Little Leigh pond, a delightful area full of wildlife. Sheep graze on the sheltered slope on the opposite bank and there is a rickety holiday cottage.

You soon come to another bridge and Daleford House. Keep along the towpath going through a kissing gate on your way to Saltersford Tunnel. Boatmen in the old days would have to leg it through this as there is no towpath to allow horses through. The old wooden posts where boats would tie up to await their turn are still visible.

Saltersford Tunnel.

Your way forward is using the old horsepath over the top of the tunnel, past a pink-painted house and through another kissing gate. There is a canal signpost here. Notice the initials of the firm that erected it on the base of the sign (R and D) and the date of 1819. There is a small air-vent tower in the field you pass and then you drop down to the canal again. Saltersford Tunnel was repaired and re-opened to canal traffic in 1984. The canal bends slightly, so the opposite end is not visible.

Go off the towpath here and follow the path up to the left into Barnton. Turn left at the main road, passing a well-stocked village store and The Beech Tree pub. After passing two garages opposite one another, turn right up Stone Heyes Lane. Pass Rosebank Farm and where the lane turns sharp left continue along it into the country.

Notice the upper storey of the barn at Stone Heys Farm. The building is now being renovated to make a house but you can clearly see where sacks were lowered from the upper storey through the gap in the wall.

Turn left just past the farm, crossing a stile and making for the electricity pylon at the far side of the field. There is a plank over the stream here and a stile just to the left of it. Keep the hedge on your right as you walk over the next field which was a potato field when I came this way last. Cross a stile at the end and continue forward between ponds towards Desley Heath Farm ahead. You then go through two gates and along the farm track to the road.

Turn left along the road which is signposted to Runcorn. As you go around the bend (!) you turn right off the road and go over a stile into a field. Make for the top right-hand corner diagonally opposite you. Go over a stile and straight across the next field to the bridge over the stream. After bearing left over the bridge you turn left at Blue Grass Animal Hotel and continue to the road and your car.

AROUND LOWER WHITLEY

Route: Chetwode Arms - Whitley Hall - Merryfall Wood - Back Lane - Village Lane

Distance: 2 to 3 miles

Start: Opposite the Chetwode Arms in Lower Whitley village (SJ 615789)

By Car: Take the A533 north west from Northwich. Turn right at the A49. Turn right into Lower Whitley and park anywhere in or near the village where it is safe to do so.

You may spot the old AA sign on the long barn opposite the pub. The faded information tells you that you are 177.5 miles from London but I hope that you will not end up walking that far today! The Chetwode Arms used to be the meeting place for the hunt and the footpath you want leads off opposite its entrance. The path skirts the churchyard, the church itself dating from the 17th century with a glorious Jacobean, hammerbeam roof.

Cross the stile at the end of this path and make your way diagonally across the small meadow to another stile in the far corner. Turn right and walk around the field until you come to another stile in the hedge. Cross it and follow the hedge down to a gate. The cart-track will then lead you to Whitley Hall.

Just before the farmhouse you turn left into a field and walk around two sides of the garden. You then climb over the fence into another field. Make for the area of reeds, keeping it on your left. It is a reed-fringed pond abounding with wild life. As you walk around this you will see a stile in the hedge ahead beside another small pond.

Continue through the next field, keeping the hedge on your right. I was accompanied along here by a carthorse and her foal. Go through the gap

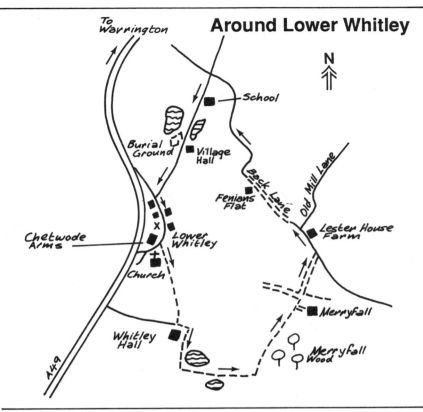

in the facing hedge and skirt around the side of the next field towards Merryfall Wood. When I did this walk in early June many of the fields were green with bearded barley waving in the breeze.

Walk up the side of the wood, admiring the pink campion and other wild flowers that abound. At the end of the wood keep straight on. You will probably find it easier to keep the hedge on your left. Merryfall is straight ahead, and when you reach it bear left along the rough road. Turn left when you come to a T-junction and this will bring you to Lester House Farm.

After passing this you turn left into Back Lane. Old Mill Lane goes to the right here. You walk along a very rough track which then becomes a tarmac road. On the left you will pass a dwelling now called Poacher's

Cottage. It used to be called Fenian's Cottage. Behind the cottage is a flat piece of land hemmed in by banks on all sides. In the olden days cattle used to be driven from Ireland to Liverpool and this area made a convenient overnight stop. The drover who used this route was called Fenian and the land now has the name of Fenian's Flat.

Lower Whitley Primary School.

Keep on along this road, passing Whitethorns with its unusual box bearing the words 'Washington Post'. Presumably this is used to keep the daily paper dry. When you reach Village Lane turn left. The attractive primary school dates from 1875.

Opposite the village hall is a sandstone wall. Over this is Frandley burial ground - a peaceful spot. You will soon reach the rest of the village. As you return to your car notice the pretty white cottages built in typical Cheshire style.

AROUND PLUMLEY

Route: Trouthall Lane - Peover Eye - Holford Moss - Langford Farm - Holford Hall

Distance: 2 to 3 miles

Start: Trouthall Lane, Plumley (SJ 717753)

By Car: Take the A556 from Northwich driving east towards Manchester. Turn right at The Smoker, a pub dating from Elizabethan times and named after a famous racehorse. The road is signposted to Plumley. Turn right at the Methodist Church down Trouthall Lane. After this bends to the left park opposite a large brick barn.

The route covered by this walk seems to be a popular one as I met several people exercising dogs, children, or simply themselves, and this was the morning of a weekday.

Walk back to Brookside Cottage, a charming, thatched dwelling, and turn down a 'No Through Road'. Cross over Peover Eye and turn immediately right over a tiny stile. The path is easily visible as it goes up the field to a large gap in the hedge. Turn right after entering the next field, but bear off left down another grassy track immediately after meeting the track to Holford Hall.

Turn left between small ponds and the path then goes ahead across the field and up over the railway line. You then continue forward along the side of a field, past small ponds. Cross a stile and continue along the next field to reach a cattle grid on a farm road. Turn left along this, past more ponds and brambles, to cross another cattle grid. Keep ahead to pass a cottage with a small Christmas tree plantation beside it.

Turn right here over a stile into a wood known as Holford Moss. At one time large areas of Cheshire were covered by peaty tracts of land. Much of this land was gradually reclaimed. Mosses, moors or heaths, often along river valleys covered with peat, were frequently used as common pasture and places where people would dig turves for their fires before coal became cheap. On this part of the walk you can feel the soft peaty

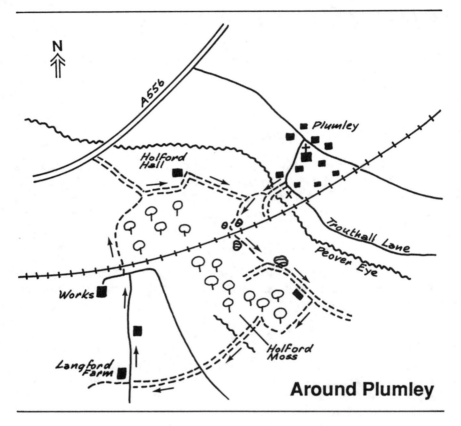

Around Plumley

texture of the soil underfoot as you negotiate the brambly path to walk through a mixed woodland, with holly and silver birch particularly predominating.

The full magic of the area is felt when the sunlight filters through the branches, and you stay on this path as it winds on through the wood. The roughly-hewn handrail of silver birch trunks shows that you are still on the right path. You eventually drop down a few rough steps and bear left to cross a stream and then walk up the side of a field.

Keep ahead when you come to a merging of tracks and ahead again when you cross the tarmac road to some works. When you reach Langford Farm, with a view of ICI in the distance, turn right. You soon

Holford Hall.

pass Hame Farm and then another works, this time almost deserted, to turn left at the T-junction. Turn right almost immediately to cross the railway line with extreme caution.

Go forward alongside a magnificent beech hedge and when the way forks turn right. Holford Hall comes into view, looking like a miniature Little Moreton Hall with its half-timbered appearance. It probably dates from the 16th century when the oak timbers of its frame would be blackened by pitch or tar to contrast with the white-washed wattle-and-daub or brick infilling. The path bends around to give you a closer look.

After passing a red gate, turn right down a cart-track that soon leads into a field. Keep along this track until you join up with the early part of your walk and return to your car.

EAST OF RUNCORN

Daresbury
Hatton
Preston Brook
Preston-on-the-Hill

The map that you need in the Pathfinder series for these walks is Widnes - Sheet SJ48/58. Travelling instructions are given from Warrington. The four walks take between one and two hours to complete and are two to three miles long.

At Norton Priory you can see the recently excavated remains of an Augustinian Abbey dating from the 12th century. There is a model of what the Abbey looked like then, plus the remains of a mosaic floor with the kiln where the tiles were made. You can wander through the informal gardens and woodland glades at will, and you will probably see two surviving summer houses.

AROUND DARESBURY

Route: Daresbury village - Keckwick Hill - Bridgewater Canal - Keckwick Lane - Daresbury Church

Distance: 2 to 3 miles

Start: Outside Daresbury church (SJ 581828)

By Car: Take the Chester road from Warrington which soon becomes the A56. Turn left into the village of Daresbury and park by the Church.

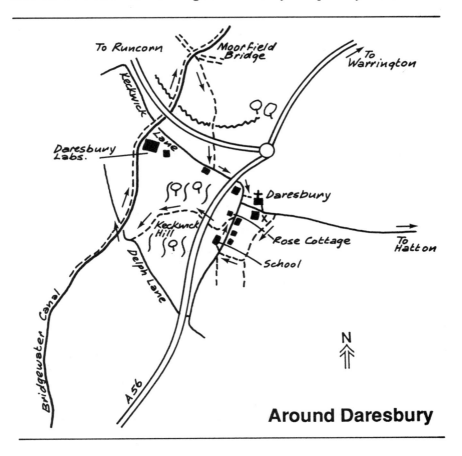

Around Daresbury

Daresbury is well known for its associations with Lewis Carroll. His real name was Charles Lutwidge Dodgson. He was the son of a Vicar of Daresbury and spent part of his childhood here. One wonders if this was where his imagination was first kindled into giving odd personalities to rabbits, caterpillars, snails and other creatures.

You will see a footpath sign a little way past the vicarage on the Hatton road. Turn right here and cross the field diagonally. The stile you are aiming for is in the far right-hand corner. Walk up the right-hand side of the next field until you come to a stile in the hedge. Turn right over this and go straight ahead keeping the hedge on your right until you reach the road.

Turn right down the road past the primary school. It must be one of the oldest ones still in use in Cheshire, dating from 1600, and its outside toilets must be the coldest! The 'Alice in Wonderland' weather vane was made by a local blacksmith and was originally erected on the chimney of the smithy. Later, however, it was donated to the school.

Turn left along the footpath just before Rose Cottage. Can you see the grinning Cheshire cat built into the barn opposite? Keep round the left-hand side of the field and cross over the stile, dual carriageway and facing stile into a field the other side of this busy road.

Go straight ahead keeping the hedge on your left until you come to another stile. This leads you over Keckwick Hill, with superb views as you follow the sign that points down to Delph Lane. Turn left when you come to a broad ride and then take the right fork. You are now passing through a plantation of evergreens which give way to silver birches before you leave the hill over a stile.

Keep to the left of the field until you leave it by the gate. Turn right along the road to the Bridgewater Canal. Cross the canal bridge and turn left along the towpath towards Daresbury Nuclear Physics Laboratory. This was opened by Harold Wilson in 1967, and its neat appearance and well-kept grounds are impressive.

Pass under two bridges. Then leave the towpath at Moorefield Bridge, crossing it and squeezing through the gap between the old post and the gate on your right. The line of the footpath goes straight across the next two fields, although it does meander somewhat after crossing the stile into the second field. When you reach the hedge at the top of this field turn right along it and you will soon come to the small stream that runs parallel to the new road. Cross it using the grassy bridge and make for the steep steps up to the road. An identical set take you down to the field on the other side. Go diagonally over this, walking up the slope, and emerge through a large gap in the hedge at the far corner onto Keckwick Lane.

Turn left, cross the dual carriageway and go down the road to Daresbury. Turn left through a tiny gate before a bus stop. Cross over a small field and go through a 'kissing gate' into the churchyard, sombrely shaded by yew trees.

The Church is well worth a visit, and is usually open on weekend afternoons. The Jacobean pulpit is beautifully carved and the Lewis Carroll Memorial Window in a side chapel depicts the author with Alice and several of the animals from his famous stories. Can you spot the White Rabbit and the Mad Hatter; and the Dormouse is there, sitting in the teapot? There are others too.

AROUND HATTON

Route: Common Side Farm - Row's Wood - Outer Wood - Hall Lane - Daresbury Lane

Distance: 2 to 3 miles

Start: On Daresbury Lane near the turn to Common Side Farm (SJ 593826)

By Car: Take the A49 from Warrington and turn right at Stretton traffic lights. When you get to the village of Hatton turn left down Daresbury Lane. Park on the grass verge on the left, just before the footpath sign to the right.

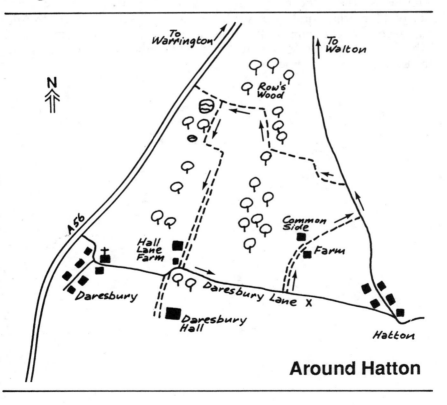

Around Hatton

Walk down the road to Common Side Farm, turning right behind the farmhouse and going through the facing gate. The grassy track ahead will bring you down to the road that runs from Hatton to Walton.

Turn left along this road for a short while. Climb the first stile you come to and walk down to the end of the hedge in front of you. Cross over the stile hidden behind it. Walk along the side of this field keeping the hedge on your right, and cross the stile into another field.

Follow the narrow 'rabbit track' straight across this long field, and where it peters out you will see a stile into Row's Wood. Go into the wood and cross the bridge over the stream. (Take care here as the plank may be very slippery.) Follow the track over to the right and out of the wood. Look out for pheasants around here.

Walk around the edge of the field keeping the wood on your right. At the corner the track rises over the hill - signposted Chester Road. You will have a good view of industrial Warrington as you reach the brow of this hill. In the daytime the overall impression is of belching smoke, but one can imagine the lights glittering like fairytale palaces at night.

Continue over to the next wood where the duck population on the pond is worth a look. But do not venture too close. There is a very explicit sign which says, 'Keep out. Trespassers may be accidentally shot!' Go around to the left, skirting this wood until you cross a stile.

The squat tower of Daresbury Church can be easily seen now. This is the oldest part of the church and dates from the 16th century. There is a ground floor ring of eight bells and an unusual rhyme to be found in the ringers' chamber. The initial letters of each line spell out the word DARESBURY. The church clock too has been equipped with Westminster chimes which add further charm to walking in this area.

The buildings of Daresbury Hall, which is a training centre for adult spastics, come into view ahead as you go round the left-hand side of the field. When you reach a gate go through it into Hall Lane. Along here the concrete tower at Daresbury Laboratory dominates the landscape, and the clock on the wooden tower of the first farm building will tell you how long you have been walking.

You will soon reach the rest of Hall-lane Farm, and the raucous noise of rooks will greet you as you turn left into Daresbury Lane and return to your car.

Daresbury Lane.

AROUND PRESTON BROOK

Route: Red Brow Lane - Crows Nest - Delph Lane - Bridgewater Canal - Preston Brook

Distance: 2 to 3 miles

Start: Behind The Lord Daresbury on Red Brow Lane (SJ 571817)

By Car: Take the Chester road out of Warrington. Just before you pass The Lord Daresbury hotel on the A56 turn right down Red Brow Lane. Park as near into the side of the road as you can.

This is a walk for striding out as the wind whips across the hillside and the large area of waste grassland between the canals and the railways. There are also some steep scrambles onto canal banks.

Stand at the top of the hill with your back to 'The Lord Daresbury'. Where a lane goes off to the left, the right-of-way for walkers goes to the right. Walk through the gap into the field. Keep along the brow of the hill with the fence on your left until you cross a stile in this and a facing stile. Keep forward to a further stile, then drop down the hill to the right of Crows Nest. Cross a stream and two stiles to the farm track where you turn right. Then turn left along Delph Lane.

Cross the canal bridge and turn left along the canal bank away from the Daresbury Laboratories. You soon come to George Gleaves Bridge, which is very old with its original stone and brick work. You can even see clear rope scores on its wooden baulks.

While walking along here you have a clear view across to Halton. From the late 12th century onwards, a stone castle stood on the hilltop there, guarding the ford over the Mersey at Runcorn. However, by the reign of Queen Elizabeth I it was only used as a prison, and it was later

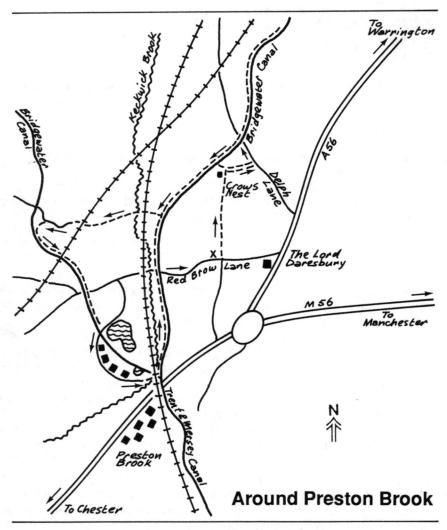

Around Preston Brook

completely destroyed, after a siege, 1643-46, by Cheshire Parliament
soldiers, probably under the local commander, Colonel Henry Brooke of
Norton Priory.

Keep your eyes open for the path that drops off the towpath and crosses
a field. Follow this under the railway bridge and cross Keckwick Brook

Canal at Preston Brook.

by a wooden bridge. From here make for the railway arches ahead and slightly to the right. Go under these and turn left along the road. Just before the road rises to go over the Bridgewater Canal take a narrow path and climb onto the canal bank.

Turn left along the towpath going under a railway bridge and a road bridge before you cross the next road bridge and turn left onto the service road behind the tall houses. You are now entering Preston Brook, a place which has grown up at the junction of roads, railways and canals. You will see glimpses of the brightly-painted canal barges moored at the marina on your left.

Just past here you come to the place where the Bridgewater Canal does a right-angled turn and the Trent-and-Mersey Canal joins it. The large warehouses at the marina used to be full of goods waiting to be transferred from the narrow boats that plied up and down the Trent-and-Mersey to the wide barges that travelled on the Bridgewater and vice-versa.

Turn left where the Bridgewater Canal appears to 'end', go under the railway bridge and then scramble up over the iron bridge to your left which brings you back onto the canal bank. Turn left and continue until you reach Red Brow Lane again. You will notice the old signal box and the signalman's cottage here. Climb up the hill as the road dips between huge rocks of sandstone, and you will soon arrive back at your car after an invigorating walk.

AROUND PRESTON-ON-THE-HILL

Route: New Manor Farm - Pear Tree Farm - Morphany Lane - (Plaque to show where Lewis Carroll was born) - Hallamhall Farm - Summer Lane

Distance: 2 to 3 miles

Start: On Summer Lane near Little Manor Farm (SJ 580810)

By Car: Leave Warrington on the A49. Turn right at Stretton traffic lights. Take the next left turn, which takes you over the motorway. Turn right onto Summer Lane and park on the verge by the entrance to Little Manor Farm.

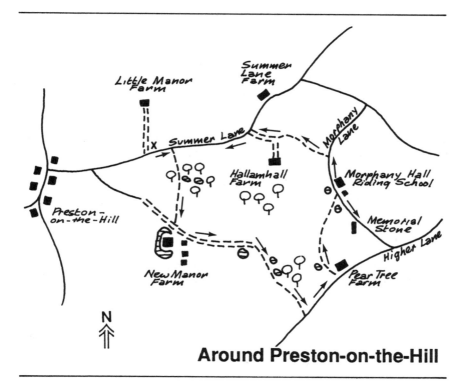

Around Preston-on-the-Hill

If you choose a clear day, this is a bright, breezy walk. It starts back at the footpath sign. Climb over the stile and go ahead keeping the hedge on your right. You will have to jump over the small stream at the bottom of the field, climb over the rickety fence, feel your way gingerly through the brambles and cross the stream again. After completing this assault course, continue forward, keeping the hedge on your right. When the hedge finishes you continue straight ahead to the stile and the road to New Manor Farm.

The farmhouse is moated - a feature of many Cheshire farms, designed more to keep out the local burglar rather than armies. Do not go through the arch to the main farm buildings but keep left along the track which leads to a small copse, where there may be farm machinery and a heap of silage. There is a clear tractor line from here across the field to the next wood. Keep to the right around this wood, and at the corner cross the field ahead keeping to the left of the small pond. You will soon come to a stile in the hedge. Cross this, and the facing stile, which brings you onto the road.

Turn left, and left again over the stile in front of Pear Tree Farm. Cross the field ahead, keeping the pond on your left. The cows are nosy but amiable. There should be a right of way through the hedge ahead but you may need to take a slight detour through the gate. Be very careful to shut this again. There is a very noticeable 'rabbit track' that runs diagonally in front of you. When it stops continue forward, negotiating the tatty barbed wire in the middle of the field. You may be lucky enough to see a hare race across the field in huge leaps and bounds.

You then make for the broken fencing in the middle of the hedge ahead. You have to choose the best place to negotiate this, which is difficult but not impossible. Slither over the stream and keep forward with the hedge on your right. I think the farmer has chosen to ignore the fact that this is a right of way. At the end of the field you have to go through the gate on the left onto Morphany Lane. Opposite is Morphany Hall Riding School, and at the duckpond beside you noisy geese may object to your arrival.

The way is really to the left along this road but if you make a detour to the right you will come to a stone which has been put up to commemorate the site of the parsonage where Lewis Carroll was born.

He actually refers to it in one of his poems called 'Three Sunsets' which is quoted on the plaque,

> "An island farm, midst seas of corn,
> Swayed by the wandering breath of morn,
> The happy spot where I was born..."

You will then have to retrace your steps before turning left off Morphany Lane at a footpath sign. Keep the fence on your right and cross two fields. You will come to the farm road leading to Hallamhall Farm. Turn right along this. When you come to Summer Lane turn left and walk back to the car.

EAST OF ELLESMERE PORT

Acton Bridge
Alvanley
Delamere
Frodsham
Kingsley

The Pathfinder map needed for these walks is Ellesmere Port (East) - Sheet SJ47/57. Travelling instructions are given from Chester. The walks vary between three and six miles, Frodsham being the shortest and Kingsley the longest. Acton Bridge and Alvanley are both about five miles and Delamere is slightly shorter, but you could combine a visit to the Delamere Visitors' Centre, which you pass en route.

For visitors to the area, the Ellesmere Boat Museum has been established where the Shropshire Union Canal ends at the Manchester Ship Canal. It is open from Easter to September and recreates a traditional canal port. It has a large collection of canal and river boats, kept in full working order wherever possible, and gives a fascinating insight into the history of this mode of transport.

Frodsham Market takes place every Thursday and people come from all over the area to trade there. Chester Zoo is nearby too with a large variety of animals, and pretty gardens.

AROUND ACTON BRIDGE

Route: Acton Brook - Acton Bridge - River Weaver - Dutton Locks - Cliff Lane - Acton Cliff - Crowton

Distance: 5 miles

Start: Near Birch House (SJ 585745)

By Car: Take the A54 from Chester and turn left onto the A49 towards Warrington. Turn left at the Hanging Gate pub at Weaverham onto the B5153 to Acton Bridge station. Keep on the road to Crowton from here and park on the right-hand side where the road has a parking space just past Birch House.

Walk back along the road and turn left along a pot-holed road sign-posted Acton Bridge. The mass of Frodsham Hill is clearly visible as you walk along between two neatly clipped hawthorn hedges. You soon come to Acton Brook, artificially widened here to make a large pleasant pool. The water overflows noisily on its way to the River Weaver.

River Weaver Swing Bridge.

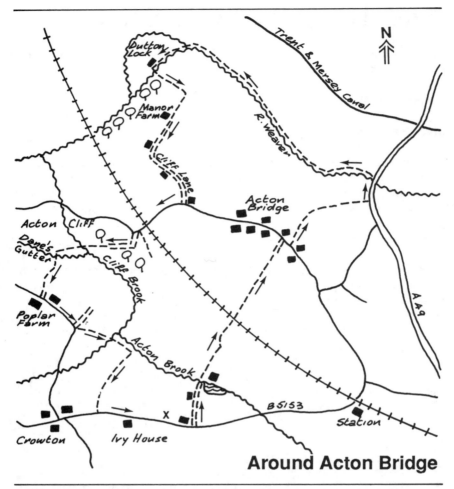

Around Acton Bridge

Keep on past a clump of bamboo. A yellow arrow shows the way over two stiles, the second leading to a field where a donkey may be in residence. Carry on along the left-hand side of the field and turn left over the stile in the corner. Keep ahead here, passing the telegraph pole, the tree and the end of the hedge and then turning right alongside this to walk towards the busy railway line ahead.

Cross the railway line with care. It is a main line and trains are frequent. Carry straight ahead across the long field in front of you. The way stretches out like a narrow ribbon and the houses of Acton Bridge village come into view. Cross the stile between two gates and keep ahead, again with the hedge on your left, to cross a stile leading to a grassy track that drops down to the road.

Turn right and immediately left between a house and a bungalow to cross a stile and drop down the field ahead. You can pick out the line of the River Weaver in the distance and the swing bridge taking the A49 over it. During the next part of the walk you are making for this bridge.

With the hedge on your left, drop down the steep part of the field, keeping a sharp eye open for rabbits in the sandy soil of the steep bank. You then cut across the marshy ground to the far right-hand corner where there is a sturdy bridge over a stream. Keep the hedge on your left until it cuts away, when you go ahead over a dyke and through any of the large gaps in the hedge. Make for an iron stile in the hedge at the far side of the next small field and you will then see steps leading up onto the A49. You will probably be glad to leave this low lying marshland, which can be extremely wet and boggy.

Turn left along the main road. There is no need to cross over as there is a wide, grassy verge and then a footpath over the bridge on this side. Turn left and drop down off the road once you have crossed the river and walk along the tarmac towpath towards Frodsham.

The River Weaver used to be a much busier waterway than it is today. Barges and sea-going vessels carried the salt traffic from Winsford to Liverpool and then on to other parts of the world. Continue along the towpath until you come to Dutton Locks. You can see how the river has been straightened considerably here. A white bridge comes into view ahead and you turn left over it.

Cross the river at the lock and follow the footpath sign away from the river but keeping the trees on your right. As you come into a field keep the hedge on your left and the hill on your right. Climb the stile at the end of the field and turn right along the muddy cart track to Manor Farm. A large, mossy boulder helps to form a stile at the end of the track which takes you into the farmyard and another mossy stone takes you over another stile out of it.

Keep ahead along the road to Willow Cottage and Weaver Holt. The name of this road is Cliff Lane which you will discover when you come to the T-junction and turn right. The road drops down under the railway line and you then turn left down the cart-track just after this. Keep on this track as it bears right up the hill passing an orchard of low-growing apple trees and then cross the stile at the end of the track.

This area is known as Acton Cliff and you can see the line of the path going straight ahead across the field. You get a good view of the many arches of Dutton viaduct from here as it takes the railway line over the River Weaver. The path drops steeply down to Cliff Brook and this can be quite treacherous.Cross the bridge and climb over the stile ahead to cross the marshy ground keeping to the left, and then crossing another stream called Dane's Gutter. I did wonder whether the large excavations here showed evidence of a badger sett. The line of alder and oak trees indicates the way to a gate out of the field and onto the road where Poplar Farm faces you.

Turn left along the road passing Yew Tree Farm, and when the road bears right you turn left and then immediately climb a stile into the field on the right. Walk straight down this field and cross Crowton Brook at the bottom of it. You then walk beside Acton Brook until you cross a stile and turn right away from it keeping the hedge on your right. You continue along here until you reach the road. Crowton village is over to your right but you turn left and pass Ivy House on your way back to the car.

AROUND ALVANLEY

Route: Alvanley - The Ridgeway - Sandstone Trail - Alvanley Cliff - Manley Old Hall - Moor's Brook - The White Lion

Distance: 5 miles

Start: Alvanley church (SJ 497741)

By Car: Take the A56 east from Chester and turn right to the village of Alvanley as you approach the outskirts of Helsby. Park near the church where the road is straight.

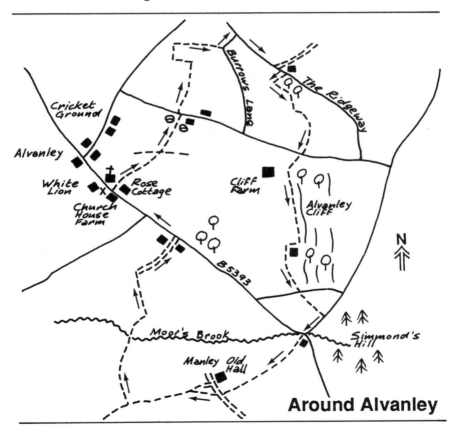

Around Alvanley

Alvanley Church Gate.

Your walk starts at the church with its tiny spire. There used to be an unusual custom carried on here called 'roping'. A rope would prevent newly-married couples from leaving the church gate before they had paid a forfeit. This would then be used by the locals to drink their health in The White Lion opposite!

Notice the Georgian building of Church House Farm, and then turn left beside Rose Cottage - now a garden centre, noted for its heathers. The raspberry canes and fruit bushes keep pace with you for some distance as you walk up this long field.

When you are almost opposite Alvanley Cricket Club, in its pleasant setting, climb over a stile into the next field. Continue in the same direction but on the other side of the hedge. Climb over another stile into a field that may have sheep in it (so keep your dog under control - if you have one), and then another one to drop down to an area between ponds.

Cross a sturdy stile between stone pillars onto the road, turn left, then immediately right, following the footpath down the edge of a field. Ahead, the industrial view of the Mersey Valley is framed by the hills of Frodsham and Helsby. The dried up stream beside you has left behind clumps of reeds lining the v-shaped valley floor.

Cross the stile at the end of the field and follow the hedge round to the left. The right of way goes round a small copse and then continues to the holly hedge ahead. Walk alongside this and turn right in front of the bridge to walk beside the stream until you reach the road. You may find this muddy in places.

Turn left down Burrows Lane. The look-out post on Foxhill Wood is very prominent. Turn right at the T-junction and continue up the hill. This road is an ancient route through these hills known as The Ridgeway. Opposite the entrance to the caravan site you go up some steps to join the Sandstone Trail. It is signposted Manley Common, Delamere Forest and Beeston Castle.

Drop through this little wood with the birds twittering merrily and turn left beside the stream. The way through here is not a public right of way and walkers are fortunate to be allowed access. The acrobatic antics of the grey squirrels in the tree-tops are often worth a second look, before you cross the bridge out of the wood.

The next part of the route follows the Sandstone Trail as you continue up the side of the field, going through the gap at the top and turning left. Motor cyclists practise scrambling on the rough, sandy ground that drops away as you keep round this field to the wooden steps down to a stile.

Timber Framed Hall - transported from Nantwich.

Carry on round the next field and Cliff Farm will come into sight, an attractive building, typical of Cheshire with its half-timber and white-wash. It is aptly named as the next part of the walk keeps under Alvanley Cliff. Cross the lane and go over the stile opposite. Walk across the grass to a stile and contine under the brow of the hill. You may see evidence of deserted sandstone quarries in the hillside, while, on the lower ground, the sandy soil often provides good crops of potatoes.

Turn right at the end of the field and then left when you pass in front of a brick and timber-framed hall, recently transported from the Nantwich area and rebuilt in this attractive setting. Cross the stile into another field and you soon come to a very unusual stile. The top arm acts as a lever as you climb over.

Cross the road and the next stile to continue in the direction of Manley Common and Delamere Forest. The path is distinct through the crops and drops down to the next lane. Turn right along this with Simmond's Hill looming beside you.

You have a choice here. If you feel that the walk has been long enough, you can turn right at the T-junction, which signifies the boundary between Alvanley and Manley, and walk along this road back to your car.

If you are game for more, go over the stile opposite, leaving the Sandstone Trail at this point. Walk down the side of the field with the hedge on your left, passing a pretty stone-built house. Fields stretch away on both sides and you may hear the local school children out at play. You can also see Alvanley nestling between the low hills that surround it.

The way drops down to Manley Old Hall. As you come to this sizable Victorian building the path crosses out of one field into the next, and continues beside a thick cupressus hedge. You then climb over a stile out of this field into the farm road.

You should really turn right to Manley Old Hall here and then left down a cart-track, but you may find yourself up to your knees or higher in cow dung so I improvised an alternative as follows!

Cross over the lane into the field ahead and turn right, dropping down the field to the water-filled quarries, prettily screened by trees. Cross out of the field onto the cart-track here and keep down this track past the two pools and then between fields to continue along a grassy track to a junction of tracks.

Turn right and walk over two fields. You can then see the stile in the hedge ahead which takes you to the bridge over Moor's Brook. Turn to the right around the side of the wood and then up the side of this field until you bear right between two large gorse bushes. Walk along the top of the rough ground here and enjoy a stunning view of the Cheshire plain.

When you reach the hedge turn left alongside a field where a root crop may be growing strongly. You soon pass an electricity pylon and come to a track where you turn right. This brings you back to the road, and you turn left, back to Alvanley village and your car.

AROUND DELAMERE FOREST

Route: Sandstone Trail - Delamere Visitors' Centre - Hart Hill - Hatchmere - Barnbridge Gates

Distance: 4 to 5 miles

Start: Barnbridge Gates car park (SJ 542716)

By Car: Take the A54 from Chester and then turn left onto the B5393, passing through Ashton before turning right for Hatchmere. Continue into Delamere Forest past Fox Howl, the outdoor education centre, and park in Barnbridge Gates car park. This landscaped gravel pit has become a bird lover's delight. Look out for wrens, nuthatches, jays and many varieties of the tit family. The birds here are so tame that even the barking of dogs does not scatter them.

Delamere Forest covers 4000 acres of Cheshire today, but many centuries ago, when the Ancient Britons camped here, it used to be three times as big. At that time it stretched all the way from Nantwich to Helsby. In the Middle Ages it was made into the twin royal forests of Mara and Mondrem.

Climb up the steps out of the car park and turn left along the Sandstone Trail - signposted Forest Visitors' Centre. Keep right, following the Sandstone Trail markers which lead you straight on at the next crossroads and at the next fork. You may be overtaken frequently on this walk by horse riders, the soft surface of the broad woodland tracks being particularly suitable for this pastime, and fallen trees often provide jumping practice too.

You soon come to the bridge over the railway. It seems incongruous to hear the hoot of a diesel in this quiet area but this is the Chester-Manchester line. Constructed in the 1870s, it is one of few lines built and owned by a committee - the Cheshire Lines Committee. It was also the last line to be brought into British Railways in 1947 - six months after the rest - due to an oversight.

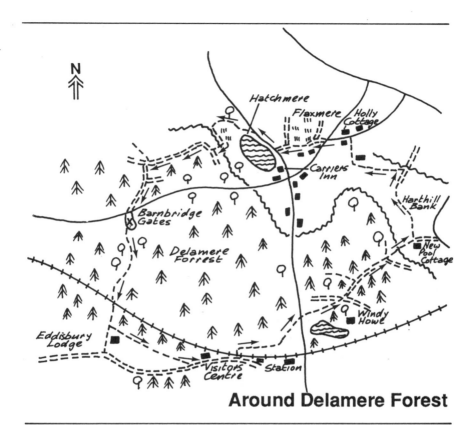

Around Delamere Forest

Leave the Sandstone Trail by bearing left just before Eddisbury Lodge. This takes its name from the hunting lodge situated here when the forest provided sport for the nobility. Continue along this path until you come to a tarmac road when you turn left again.

A ridge of hills rolls away nearby. The summit of Eddisbury Hill is the highest point and the remains of an ancient fortress can be found there. You soon arrive at a Forestry Commission depot and a row of greenhouses. In front of these is a notice which tells of their use. 'Through this gate is the old Pale Nurseries. Inside the polihouses are young pines grown from seed and young spruce trees grown from cuttings. They will be sent to forests all over the United Kingdom to produce fast grown plantations of high quality timber.'

You then pass the Forestry Commission Visitors' Centre which is well worth a visit either now or on your way home. There is also a map with all the various way-marked walks through this part of the forest. For the next part of this walk you are going to follow the yellow arrows with the green spot.

Just past here, after signs warning of the danger of electricity pylons, turn left to re-cross the railway and then immediately drop off the track on your right and walk through the wood parallel with the railway line. When you reach the station, with its cottages for railway employees, the path veers to the left. The leaf mould underfoot provides a soft surface for one's long-suffering feet as you pass a scrubby field of grass, and then an area composed of both the natural forest of deciduous trees and the artificially introduced evergreens for the forestry industry.

When you come to the road cross over it and continue towards Norley. An expanse of water shimmers up through the trees and Windy Howe sits on the hillside. You come to clearings dominated by massive beech trees, their horizontal branches guarding their territory. These give way to younger beeches on either side of the path, the tangle of their roots so shallow that they often protrude above the surface and are easy to trip over.

Turn right onto a much wider track to keep ahead past plantations both new and old. As you climb out of a valley you come to a junction of paths where you bear slightly to the left up over the hill. This brings you out of the main wood, and you keep ahead between rough fields, low-lying and marshy.

When you come to New Pool Cottage turn left over a stile to walk down a grassy track furrowed by tractor tyres. The hillside, with its tussocks of grass, and small beech trees struggling for existence, is called Harthill Bank. Cross a small stream and then a stile, still following the green-dotted arrows. They are even painted on trees where the direction may be confusing.

Bear left over a small hill and you can see the path ahead to a facing hedge. Turn right as you reach this hedge and walk along it, crossing a stile into a field which may have bullocks in it. Keep along the hedge, over another stile out of the field and onto the grassy track again.

This leads down into a small valley. Keep your eyes skinned as there is a stile in the hedge before you cross the stream. It is rather rickety and gives the impression of being little used, but it is an authorised right-of-way. Climb over it and walk parallel to the stream along the bottom of the field until you come to a step-ladder stile with most of the steps missing. It isn't too difficult to negotiate though! Continue along the hawthorn hedge, a haven for tiny birds which twitter ahead of you.

As you approach the farmyard there is an area of sludge to cross near the cow byre before you turn right onto the farm track. A clean puddle might be available here to splash the cow muck from your boots! Bear left at the brick barn over a stile into a field. Keep alongside the hedge to the road and turn left.

Turn left along the road to pass aptly-named Holly Cottage and when you reach the fork continue ahead down 'No Through Road'. Where this track splits go ahead again bearing left. The area of land over to the right is called Flaxmere. It used to be a lake in the 13th century but is now reduced to a sunken moss. The track finishes at a cottage dated 1833, with the builder's initials for all to see.

Your way now continues down a tiny path until you turn left down a dirt road as reed-fringed Hatchmere comes into view. There is a car-park and toilets here, opposite the Carriers Inn where there has been a pub for over 300 years.

Turn right along the B5152 and where the mere ends turn left along a path. Keep on this path as it takes you away from the lake to the edge of the forest, through bracken and grassy clearings. When you are stopped by a facing stream turn left alongside it. The area here may be boggy as you follow the stream until you reach a wooden bridge over it.

Cross this and go straight up the hill ahead which brings you onto a broad forest road. Turn right along this. Although there are some enticing small paths through the trees, keep on this main track, turning right when you come to another wide track. Its grassy border and soft surface, strewn with pine needles, leads you to the edge of the forest and a field on your right.

At the end of this field ignore a tempting stile, and turn back into the forest. Keep ahead, ignoring other paths, and this broad track will soon bring you back to the car-park.

AROUND FRODSHAM

Route: Shepherd's Cottage - Beacon Hill - Sandstone Trail - Dunsdale Hollow - Woodhouse Hill Fort - Snidley Moor - Riley Bank

Distance: 3 miles

Start: Lay-by near Riley Bank (SJ 519747)

By Car: Take the A56 east from Chester. In the centre of Frodsham turn left onto the B5152. Turn right after a mile onto the Manley road and travel about a mile. Park in a small lay-by on the left after passing Shepherd's Cottage.

The road walking is completed at the beginning of this walk and your circulation will be improved quickly as you walk back up the hill. After passing Shepherd's Cottage turn left over the stile into a field. There are excellent views of the industrial belt along the Mersey for much of this walk. The word 'Mersey' means 'river at the boundary' and this waterway used to form a natural boundary line between Lancashire and Cheshire.

Bear right across this field towards the radio masts on the summit of Beacon Hill. Cross the high step-ladder stile which drops into the farm lane and then continue ahead over the criss-cross stile and along the facing path. Keep along this sheltered path with views opening out to the north-east. Daresbury tower and the Runcorn water tower are prominent landmarks as you cross another stile and continue ahead along the edge of a field.

When you arrive at the road turn left to pass Beacon Hill and the start of the Sandstone Trail. For the next part of this walk you will be following the Sandstone Trail markers, defined by a footprint with the letter 'S' on them.

Turn left down a cart track and the sandstone crag of Helsby Hill rears up ahead. Fiddlers Ferry power station belches out smoke to vie with the petro-chemical complex at Stanlow. Motorways, canals, bridges, fly-

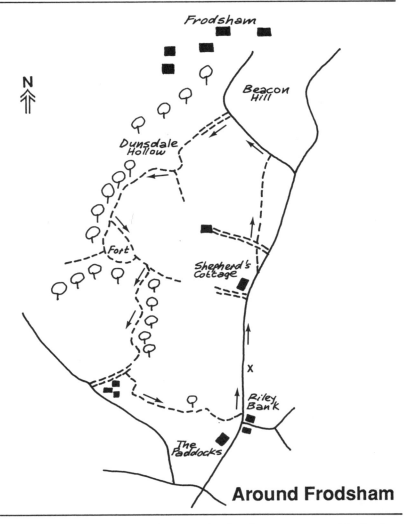

Around Frodsham

overs and railways spread-eagle over the landscape to provide further evidence of the Industrial Age.

When the track ends in a field keep straight on with the hedge on your left. Pass between gorse bushes and brambles to drop down into the steep, wooded valley of Dunsdale Hollow. There is a severe drop on

Jacob's Ladder.

your right but man-made and sandstone steps bring you safely down into this. Don't miss the encouraging sign saying 'NOTSOFARNOW' before you turn back to Jacob's Ladder. This was the original way down into the hollow. Bear left here to clamber out of the other side of the valley by means of more, huge sandstone steps, conveniently formed by the weathered rock, and known locally as Abraham's Leap.

The Sandstone Trail continues along the top of the hill. The small town of Helsby comes into view nestling under its forbidding hill, and you can see how the drained marshland around it is now used for agriculture. Go ahead at the next fork, keeping below the brow of the hill until you arrive at a viewpoint from a flat sandstone slab - a delightful place for a picnic in summer.

You can go either way around Woodhouse Hill Fort at the next fork. It is one of seven forts along the sandstone ridge of west Cheshire and dates from as far back as the Iron Age. All that is left of the settlement is an earth mound but the early families would have lived in huts, sheltered from the weather by the tree-covered hillside, and with a good vantage point from which to spot sudden danger.

The path to the left of the fort can get muddy, but from it you walk beside a field until Sandstone Trail signs tell you to bear right. The path then shelters again below the brow of the hill, becoming sandy underfoot in places. Bear left, with fields on one side, while bracken and rhododendrons cover the hillside on the other. Evidence of rabbits, badgers and foxes can be found in the sandy banks as you continue along this broad, sandy track until the trees on your left finish.

At the end of the first field you come to a gate with a pretence at a stile beside it. Turn left here and walk up through the field beside a pond. This has formed recently as there is a blockage preventing the water draining away naturally under the Trail and into the valley below. (If you reach the caravan site you have missed this turn and will need to retrace your steps.)

When you reach a stile at the top of the field turn right into a short cart track which may be extremely muddy. You come to another stile at the end of this. Do not go over it but turn left along the bracken-strewn hillside. The valley you are now in is an unspoilt, natural delight. Bear right after climbing a stile. This will bring you to a stepladder stile.

The house which comes into view here dates from 1450 and at one time it was owned by a French abbot. It is an immaculate farmhouse now, surrounded by freshly-painted, white fences with gates to match. Immediately after negotiating this stile, climb up a steep path to the left which brings you out of the valley and into a field. Keep ahead, making for the signpost on the road ahead. Climb the stepladder stile out of the field and turn left along the road back to your car.

AROUND KINGSLEY

Route: Peel Hall - Hatley Farm - Beechmill - Bradley Orchard - Frodsham Cut - River Weaver - Catton Hall - Kingsley church

Distance: 6 miles

Start: Near the church at Kingsley (SJ 547750)

By Car: Take the A56 from Chester. In the centre of Frodsham turn right onto the B5152. Turn left off this onto the B5153. Park on the right just before you pass the church at Kingsley. You should be able to get the car off the road here.

There is a footpath sign on the opposite side of the road. Cross to it and climb the steep steps to the field above. Keep the hedge on your right and follow it around until you cross the stile into the next field. Carry on in the same direction with the land dropping away to give a wide, sweeping view. Drop down out of this field onto a pebbly drive which leads to a country lane. You turn slightly to the right along this and then left over another stile off the road.

There are tracks to either side but you go straight down and over the stream. The planks forming the bridge are quite high but a sturdy handrail now helps to prevent vertigo. The stile on the opposite side says, 'Landowners welcome caring walkers. CLA - Country Landowners' Association'. Let us hope we keep it that way. This is a pretty valley, with the stream bubbling below, but you continue over the stile, and along the path to another stile. When you come to the grassy cart-track turn right up the hill.

You soon go over a stile at the end of the track into a field and, keeping the hedge on your right, continue towards Peel Hall. This is a farmhouse built on the site of a much older moated grange. Go over the stile out of this field and into the farm lane, turning left away from the buildings.

When you come to a T-junction go across the road and down the cart track opposite. This takes you down the side of a field, over a stile and past a small sewage works humming as it operates! Continue across this

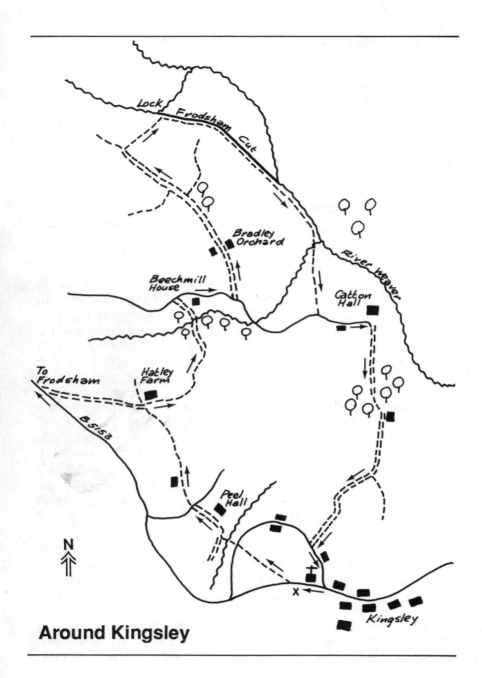

Around Kingsley

field on the cart track. Keeping the hedge on your left continue around the next field until you come to the footpath sign to the left of the farm. Cottages on the outskirts of Frodsham nestle under the hill.

Turn right towards the farm, passing the old water pump in the garden. Make your way through the farmyard and over the stile at the end of it to drop down the field keeping the hedge on your right. Cross the stile into the next field and turn left into the one adjacent to it. Drop down this field diagonally until you come to a stile in the facing hedge. Climb over this and turn left along a farm track.

There is evidence of old orchards throughout this area. Cross the stream in its steep valley, the waterfalls dropping noisily away, and you soon come to Beechmill House. This is built on the site of the original mill. Turn right at a newly-tarmaced road to drop down the hill. Almost at the bottom of this turn left towards Bradley Orchard along a stony track. The way continues to the left of the farmhouse and winds its way up the hill.

The railway viaduct and the M56 span the wide valley ahead - feats of engineering from different centuries. The hillside drops away steeply beside you and when you come to the fork take the left turn over the stile ahead. Keep left across the field and follow this track over the next field. Pass the beech and hawthorn hedge at the end and make a right-angled turn alongside it.

You are now dropping down to the River Weaver with the stream beside you all the way. Turn right at Frodsham Lock to walk on the towpath alongside Frodsham Cut. This was an improvement made to the river in the 18th century which is now no longer used. A bridge so low that even a punt could not pass under it crosses to a sign stating 'Bull grazing' - a complete deterrent to venture further! Herons are often visible in the wild land around here.

The cut ends and you continue beside the main river. Hawthorn bushes stud the high banks, and sheep may be peacefully grazing in the fields beside you. When you come to a brown, iron gate go through it, or around it, to pass over a stream that enters the river here. You then go through another gate and turn away from the river to negotiate some marshy ground where drainage is in progress. After passing through a further gate walk up the side of a field to the lane, where you turn left towards Catton Hall.

There used to be a ford over the river here before it was made navigable, but you make a right-angled turn up a lane to a wood. Walk through this and continue along the track as Kingsley church comes into view ahead. Keep along here until you turn left onto a country road which brings you to the lychgate of the church. Here, you turn right up the main road and back to your car.

EAST OF CHESTER

Christleton
Eccleston
Little Budworth
Primrose Hill
Tarporley

The map in the Pathfinder series that you need for these walks is
Chester (East) - Sheet SJ46/56. Travelling instructions are given from
Chester. Tarporley and Primrose Hill are approximately six miles long,
Little Budworth is five, Christleton is four and Eccleston about three.

The motor racing circuit at Oulton Park has a meeting most weekends in
the summer months. There is also a day of vintage and veteran car
racing in June called the Richard Seaman Trophy Meeting. (Richard
Seaman was a racing driver who was killed in an accident in the 1930s.)
The Concour d'Elegance parade of old cars around the circuit before the
races begin is very impressive.

The grounds of Eaton Hall are open to the public on three afternoons
during the year, the proceeds going to charity. The chapel and old
Victorian stables are open at the same time.

There is also plenty of interest in Chester. Its Cathedral has a recently-
constructed detached bell tower and you can watch the bells being rung
for Evensong on Sunday afternoons. 'The Rows' date from the Middle
Ages and form a unique shopping precinct. A walk round the city walls
takes about two hours. Boats of various kinds can be hired for a trip on
the River Dee. Chester also has one of the oldest race courses in the
country, with meetings held during the flat racing season.

AROUND CHRISTLETON

Route: Little Heath - Rake Lane - Brown Heath Road - Shropshire Union Canal - Christleton - Littleton

Distance: 4 miles

Start: Off Little Heath Road by the swings (SJ 443659)

By Car: Take the A41 from Chester and turn left off this to Christleton. This pretty village is only two miles from Chester and wealthy merchants trading in the city built themselves houses there. You enter the village on Pepper Street, where many of the houses are Georgian. On your left, look out for a gazebo built into the walls of Christleton Hall and Christleton House. These towers, built into the garden walls of big houses, enabled ladies to see what was going on outside. Keep left at the church into Little Heath Road and turn right as you come to the pretty pond, fringed by reeds. There is an open area for parking here, by a recreation ground with swings.

Walk through the gate beside the British Legion building and keep down the side of a field to go through the narrow gap into the next field. Walk round to the left and keep left when you come to the corner. You soon reach a stile set into sandstone pillars which brings you into the next field. Walk down the long side of this rectangular field until you exit from it at a further stile between stone pillars.

Turn right at the pond here to go along a track which takes you alongside the road to a crossroads. Continue down Rake Lane towards Waverton, passing a row of terraced houses before entering Brown Heath Road at the next crossroads.

Pass a garden centre and several houses before turning right down a footpath towards Rowton Bridge. Follow the arrows on the stiles along here. Keep to the right of the first field and you will come to a pretty pond, fringed by hawthorn trees and willows. Keep ahead at the next stile, and then cross two more stiles to bring you up onto the bank of the Shropshire Union canal. Over to your left is the place where the Battle of

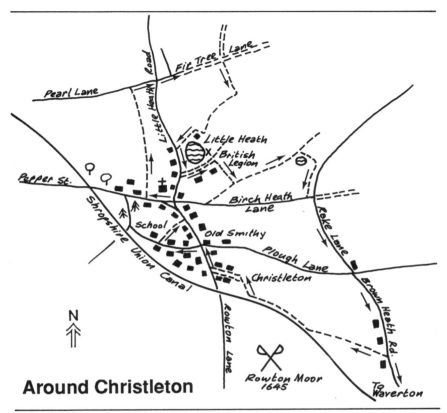

Around Christleton

Rowton Moor took place in 1645, when Charles I's army was heavily defeated.

Cross a further stile and stay on the towpath until you reach a signpost in a field. Here you bear right to go down a snicket on the far side of a grassy hummock. This leads you past a beech hedge and into Skips Lane. Look out for the cockerel weather vane as you walk down to Rowton Lane, where you turn right.

When you reach a crossroads look to your right and you will see the Old Smithy, which is still operating. Then turn left and keep on this road until you turn right down the footpath at the side of the primary school. This brings you out at Iris Cottage and you walk up past the Ring o' Bells, an old coaching inn, to the church.

On the triangle here is the old pump house, built in 1886 and carved in wood on a sandstone base. Its pump is unusually placed outside the building. The low Manor House, sited next to the church, has walls of local brick and a Tudor porch; while on the opposite corner is the Old Hall, hidden behind trees of yew and holly. It is the oldest building in the village, dating from 1605, and is surrounded by a tunnel which may once have been linked to Chester.

Christleton Church.

Turn left at the church. The oldest part of this is the 15th century tower, gargoyles hang off the four corners below the high parapet which is topped by a square lantern. The gilt clock dates from 1888 and the cockerel weather vane completes the picture.

Turn right through an iron gate beside the churchyard towards Littleton and go over a stile into a grassy field. From here you can see Christleton Hall, built in the 18th century. It is now used as a law school and dwarfed by modern extensions.

Cross another stile, a field, and a further stile to keep down the side of the next field. Cross into an adjacent one about halfway along this, and walk in the same direction until you meet the road over another stile.

Turn right down Pearl Lane, lined with gnarled oaks, and keep ahead at the crossroads, past Orchard House, to bear right down Fir Tree Lane.

After the houses have ended turn right down the side of a field over a stile. Turn right over another stile and bear right round a brick and timber house to a stile which brings you onto a rough road. Keep ahead past mossy stones engraved with sheaves of wheat - if you peer closely.

Turn left at the road and left again as you pass the bungalow with the stork weather vane. Pass the black and white almshouses, built in the last century, that look out onto the pond, and return to your car.

Christleton Almshouses.

AROUND ECCLESTON

Route: Eccleston - River Dee - Eaton Hall

Distance: 3 miles

Start: Near the church in Eccleston (SJ 414626)

By Car: Take the A483 from Chester and turn left to the village of Eccleston. Keep ahead here and park near the church.

This is a walk that may only occasionally be enjoyed to the full, as the return route is through the private grounds of Eaton Hall. These may be open to the public on Bank Holiday weekends, when all the proceeds go to charity. The first of these days, and perhaps the prettiest, may be Easter Sunday afternoon when the daffodils are in full bloom.

However, the walk by the river can be enjoyed at other times, provided that it is not in flood. And you do get different glimpses of the estate through the trees on the return route.

Eccleston itself is an interesting little village. Eaton Hall is owned by the Duke of Westminster and is part of the Grosvenor estate. Eccleston is one of the estate villages where the first Duke of Westminster built cottages to house his employees, and a church to house their souls! Many of the houses have the lower half built out of brick or sandstone, and the upper half, often gabled, has the unmistakable 'magpie' look so typical of Cheshire.

Eccleston church is beautifully maintained, with its wrought iron gates originating from Flintshire, the pillars topped by urns. The avenue of limes, looking like a row of lollipops, lead one's eye to the church itself.

The farmhouses and farm buildings dotted over the countryside all bear the unmistakable stamp of the estate and there are no less than 47 tenant farms situated locally. To see some of these, take the path down to the river towards Aldford - where it says 'No Camping'. Turn right at the river and walk beside a meadow to come to the place where there used

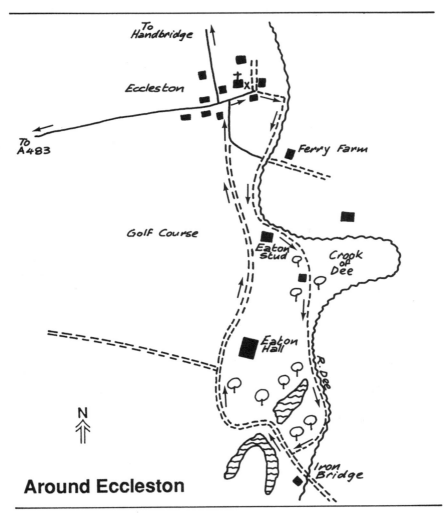

Around Eccleston

to be a ferry, and where the farm on the opposite bank still bears the name of Ferry Farm.

As you pass through a small wood, boat crews, their coxes at full throttle, may be out practising, or at the weekend there may be a Head of River race to add interest. Walk down a long flight of steps to pass a cascading waterfall, and then continue to Eaton Stud.

Bear right through a gate as you approach the Crook of Dee, a large loop of the river, and continue along a track through a wood to pass a cottage fronted by clumps of daffodils in the spring. You catch a glimpse of a miniature Big Ben - a clock tower detached from the private chapel. The vibrant sound of its bell rings out at regular intervals. Keep ahead to meet the river once more, after passing a derelict house.

Cross a stile and the high-pitched honking of geese will accompany you past their meadow. You may have a glimpse of Eaton Hall itself and the family chapel along here. The white, flat-roofed mansion, faced with marble, was only built in the 1970s. Its modern design contrasts strongly with the Victorian chapel beside it. The stable block, too, is Victorian, and all these buildings are surrounded by superb, landscaped gardens. Capability Brown himself designed the garden behind the house.

The two bridges that come into sight offer a similar contrasting picture. The first, made of natural stone, has a simple line of graceful, low arches. The second, a suspension bridge, is made of iron, laced with intricate patterns, and painted powder blue and white. After crossing a further stile you come to a private drive. If you are retracing your steps along the river bank, the view from the bridge is worth a pause.

If it is one of the open afternoons, you can now turn right to enjoy the gardens, the old stables and the church before walking back through the grounds to your car in Eccleston. Back in the village you turn right at the pumphouse built in 1874. Many of the houses also originate from the 19th century, although the oldest one, the Manor House, dates from 1632. If you are returning to Chester on the Handbridge road, its straightness indicates its Roman origin.

AROUND LITTLE BUDWORTH

Route: Budworth Pool - Coach Road - Little Budworth Common - Oulton Mill - Dogmore Lane - Oulton Park - Little Budworth

Distance: 5 miles

Start: The east end of Little Budworth Pool (SJ 600656)

By Car: Take the A54 from Chester towards Middlewich. Turn right at the A49 and then take the first turn to the left to Little Budworth. Turn left when you reach the gates of Oulton Park motor racing circuit. Drive through the village of Little Budworth and, after rounding the bend past the church, there is a small area to park by Budworth Pool.

Walk forward and turn left at the footpath sign which takes you alongside the mere. About halfway along its length turn right over a stile. Cross the field and climb over two more stiles to turn left down a cart-track which becomes a sunken lane - a typical feature of the Cheshire countryside.

When you reach the road turn left and immediately right over a stile into a field signposted to Whitehall Lane. Yellow arrows at each stile indicate clearly which way to go along here. Walk across the field to a stile which is to the left of the white house. Turn left after crossing it to another stile. Cross this field diagonally, skirting the wood until you come to a stile in the very far corner.

Turn right for a short way up a deep sandy lane, lying snugly between banks topped by hedgerows. Then go left down a well worn track. Where this forks keep left to wind up the hill past one or two houses. Stay on this broad dirt road, ignoring all paths off it, until you come to the Coach Road. This was built in the 18th century as a long, straight drive up to the gates of Oulton Park, which was then a large estate.

Cross the road and enter a lovely stretch of common land. The sandy soil, in abundance in the large sandy clearings, has never been worthy of

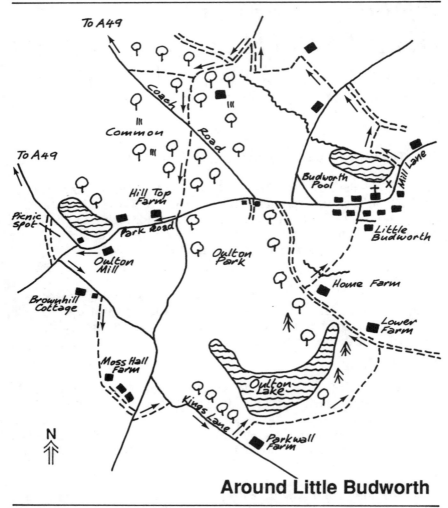

Around Little Budworth

cultivation; and the woodland, where silver birches predominate, has an almost ethereal quality. Keep on this track until you reach Park Road and turn right to Oulton Mill, passing Hill Top Farm with its equine weather vane. This is a reminder that the area has a number of stables (racing and hunting), and that the kennels of the Cheshire Hunt are only a few miles to the north. The bridleways are occasionally used for training gallops.

Oulton Mill.

The mill pool is an attractive feature and Oulton Mill has a new use - selling antiques and reproduction furniture. Climb up the hill past Mungo's Restaurant and a pleasant picnic site. Let's hope it remains that way and litter doesn't spoil it. At the crossroads here turn left towards Rushton and Wettenhall.

Immediately after passing Brownhill Cottage, a little gem dated 1675, and a tribute to the art of thatching, turn right through the steel gate into a field. Cross this diagonally keeping left and you will see a stile in the hedge. Cross the next field diagonally right. You will quickly see a stile almost halfway along the hedge. Cross this field diagonally, keeping left to the steel gate in the fence, and walk up the final field to pass the outbuildings of Moss Hall Farm. You then go through two steel gates into the farm lane, where you pass a line of poplars, perhaps acting as a wind break.

After passing Holly Bank Farm and Sunnyside Cottage you come to Dogmore Lane, where you turn right and immediately left through a gate into a field. Cross diagonally to the top right-hand corner. You may have to shoo off some extremely inquisitive bullocks all the way over this field. There should be a stile in the corner but you may have to creep under the fence.

Turn right along the road, which is Kings Lane. After passing the wood, and just before reaching Parkwall Farm, turn left through a steel gate. Walk down to the wall at the bottom of the field and turn right over a stile. You have a good view of Oulton Lake and the motor racing circuit through gaps in the wall along here. Oulton Park is one of the premier venues for motor racing in England, and there are meetings here on most weekends during the summer months.

Keep along beside the wall, crossing four more stiles, and when you reach the one by a white gate cross into the field and walk down it, keeping the hedge on your right, until you come to a steel gate. Go through this and turn left along a farm road to pass the Lower Farm of the Darley Hall estate.

Little Budworth church tower and the houses of the village come into view as you continue along here, past Home Farm with its neat buildings grouped in a rectangle round an open cobbled yard. This is a good example of the way dairy farms were built in the last century.

Enter the first field on the right after this, over a stile. Pass the telegraph pole on your right and drop down to another stile over a stream full of bright green, healthy water cress. Climb the hill out of this little valley and make for a stile between two gates ahead. Keep the fence on your left as you walk along the side of two more fields.

This brings you to the entrance to Townsfield Drive, but keep ahead down Booth Avenue to turn right at the main road. It is worth pausing to look at the church along here. The oldest part is the tower, and this is ornamented by numerous faces and gargoyles. The Red Lion also dates back to the last century, with homemade food and an unspoilt atmosphere. Shortly after this you leave Vicarage Lane and turn into Mill Lane to drop down the slope back to your car.

AROUND PRIMROSE HILL

Route: A54 - Tirley Garth - Bentley Trout Mere - Sandstone Trail - Willington Wood - Primrose Hill - Stoney Lane

Distance: 6 miles

Start: Lay-by on A556 (SJ 558684)

By Car: Take the A51 from Chester, turning left in Tarvin onto the A54. Branch left again onto the A556 towards Northwich. After passing Delamere school, about half a mile further on, park in a lay-by on the right-hand side of the road.

You pass over Primrose Hill near the beginning and the end of this walk. It is a large, detached segment of Delamere Forest and is a mixture of Scots and Corsican pines, with deciduous trees around the perimeter. Squirrels build their dreys in these, and you may see birds such as willow warblers, chiff-chaffs, tree-creepers and nuthatches.

Walk back to the stile and signpost to Quarry Bank and turn left to walk down the side of a field. Then drop down stone steps between stout stone handrails onto the A54. Cross over this busy road with care and continue towards Quarry Bank and Delamere Forest, keeping down the side of this long field and climbing the stile into the wood at the end.

The steep pull up the hill here is rewarded with a view over to the Pennines as you reach the brow of the hill. Beech trees stand to attention like soldiers on parade. Drop down the other side of the hill. The carpet of leaf mould and leaves make the ground soft underfoot. Fir trees crack and creek eerily. Many of them seem to have been damaged by heavy winds.

After crossing the start of a stream the branches of the firs reach out greedily across the path towards the light. Patches of primroses thrive where the sun's rays filter through, and you climb again beside a barbed-wire fence. This is a steep pull up to the road, passing a more recent plantation of long-needled Christmas trees.

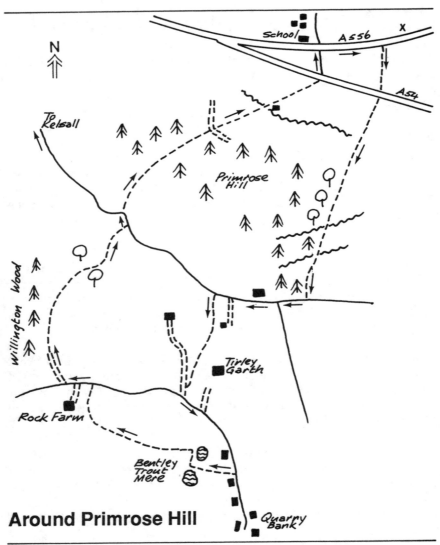

Around Primrose Hill

Turn right and carry on at the crossroads towards Kelsall, past a garden with an old-fashioned water pump. Just past the entrance to Tirley Garth turn left down a footpath signposted to John Street. You follow the blue arrows down through this pretty valley, keeping ahead for a short way and then turning left.

After passing a large shed look out for primroses and snowdrops in the early part of the year, and for rabbit holes in the soft earth. The main house comes into view as you leave the estate by a gate. Take care as you walk down the path to the road, for the bank drops away steeply beside you.

An elaborate and sturdy stile brings you out onto a lane, and you turn left away from the farm, and then left again at the road towards Utkinton. You pass the impressive, front entrance of Tirley Garth along here with its stone steps and pillars.

Keep along the road until you pass the notice advertising Bentley Trout Mere. Then turn right at the stile before the next house. Follow the yellow arrows and keep ahead over three more stiles to the mere in its pretty setting. The pools flank both sides of the path, and you climb over a further stile to leave this sheltered spot.

Extensive views open up as you turn right up the side of the field and then turn left at the dry sandstone wall ahead, its surface ingrained with moss and grass. Beeston Castle comes into view as you carry on beside the hedge, over stiles into the next field, and on in the same direction.

The Cheshire plain looks like a patterned duvet cover as it spreads out as far as the Welsh foothills. Turn right over the stile at the white gate and go up the side of the field to another white gate ahead. The radio mast high above Kelsall stands out prominently here.

Turn left along the road towards Delamere to pass Rock Farm with its brick-built barn. As the road starts to drop down the hill turn right along a wide cinder track, still following the Sandstone Trail towards Delamere. Wherever there is a sandy bank rabbit holes appear, and you pass banks of rhododendrons before the cinders give way to sand.

The evergreen strip of Willington Wood keeps pace with one a field's width away as you walk through stretches of soft sand. After passing through a coppice with sandstone outcrops, the path may become very muddy. This is caused by a spring that surfaces from underground. You continue down a sunken path between banks topped by hawthorn hedges, a typical feature of the Cheshire countryside, and there is an attractive view out between the hills.

Sunken Lane - Primrose Hill.

Turn left along the road for a short way and then right at a sharp corner to follow the Sandstone Trail marker towards Delamere Forest once more. Go down a narrow alley, and then ahead along the side of a field towards the wide sweep of Primrose Hill. Before the end of this field pass through a kissing gate and continue in the same direction, dropping down into the wood. Turn immediately right and left.

Cross over a flint road and keep forward until you leave the wood at a stile into a field. The TV mast in the distance looks as if it has a multitude of loud hailers attached. Make for the workings in the middle of the field where there is a stile, and then follow the line of telegraph poles up to a further stile. At this point cross diagonally to the right-hand corner of the field ahead where you come to a final stile and the A54.

Cross the busy road and go down the short road opposite, from which you may be able to spy your car. At the crossroads you may wish to have a closer look at the sandstone building of Delamere school, dated 1846. You may also spot the old, low signpost on the grass verge as you walk back to your car along the A556.

AROUND TARPORLEY

Route: Tarporley church - Birch Heath - Pudding Lane - Shropshire Union Canal - Sandstone Trail - Tarporley

Distance: 6 miles

Start: The car-park in Tarporley (SJ 555623)

By Car: Take the A51 from Chester. After passing the church in Tarporley look out for the signs to the free public car-park behind the Community Centre.

The land around Tarporley is ideal for dairy farming. This walk takes you across many of the small, irregular fields found in this region. Many of these have been enclosed since the 16th century. Much of the route is clearly marked by yellow arrows on the stiles.

Walk back up the main street, passing the chapel which is shared by the Baptists and Methodists. You also pass the Crown Inn, venue for the Cheshire Hunt. As you approach the church turn left through a lychgate and walk down a footpath at the side of the graveyard, signposted to Birch Heath. There are small iron gates at both ends of this path.

Leave the churchyard and keep ahead across the field, skirting work in progress on drainage ditches. Watch out for a stile overhung by a hawthorn tree in the hedge on your left. Turn right over this and shortly climb over another stile to cross the bypass and continue towards Birch Heath, which is clearly signed along the side of the field.

At the end of the hedge go left over another stile and then turn right to continue in the same direction. As you pass a gorse-fringed basin views of Beeston Castle and the hills beyond stretch away in a series of scarps and dips.

Leave the hedge and continue over the field to a stile amid a complicated fencing structure, calculated to let the walker through but not the cattle! Cross muddy tracks and go ahead to the next stile. Now

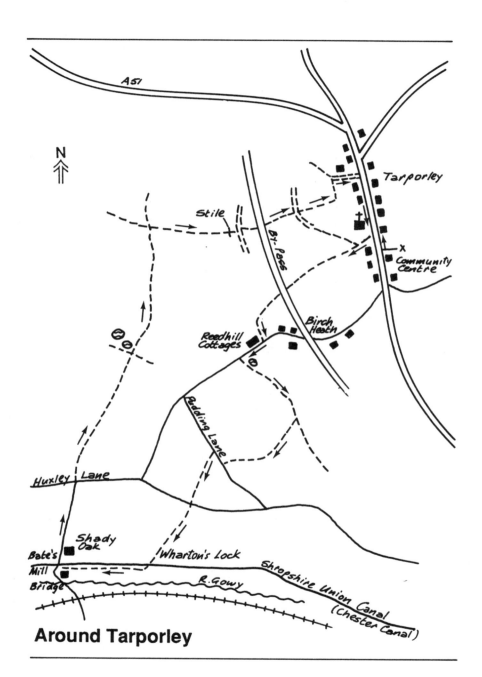

Around Tarporley

keep the hedge on your left to reach yet another stile, where you turn right along the road to pass Reedhill Cottages.

Soon after this, by a messy pond, turn left (signposted Tiverton and Beeston Brook). Skirt the pond and climb over a second stile with clumps of primroses nestling beside it. Keep along the edge of the field to a further stile, and along the edge of a second field to another stile. Bear right round the edge of this field, and keep right again beside the hedge when you come to the next one.

Cross the next stile, which is beside an iron gate, and turn right to cross this field. Keep away from the right-hand hedge and you will come to a stile in the facing hedge. Walk towards Beeston Castle as you cross the next field and come to a stile by a marl pit. Cross this and a ditch and keep near the right-hand side of the field until you cross a stile near an oak tree to bring you into Pudding Lane.

The hedges on this walk are typical of our old English countryside with trees sticking up at intervals to break the line. Turn right and immediately left over a stile towards Beeston Castle, passing a tennis court. Go over a sturdily-built stile and bridge into the next field, where the way is straight ahead. Keep ahead after crossing another stile, walking at the side of the field until you turn right in the corner to walk to the stile. Cross this and the road to follow the Sandstone Trail markers down the side of a field that rolls down to Wharton Lock.

The waterway here is the Shropshire Union canal, built in 1775 to link the Midlands to Chester. Cross over the bridge and turn right along the towpath under it, looking out for the rope marks that are clearly visible on its sides. Beeston Castle, perched in its precarious position high on its hill, looks as if it could topple off at any moment. The River Gowy and the railway run parallel to the canal here.

When you reach Bates Mill Bridge notice the original mill south of the towpath. It has been renovated for private use. Walk across the bridge here, and continue up the road past The Shady Oak pub. On reaching a T-junction keep ahead over a stile into a field. You cross this bearing to your right until you reach a stile in the facing hedge. Keep to the right again over the next field towards a well-made stile in the far corner.

Keep ahead over this field to a flimsy plank bridge over a ditch. Then ahead again bearing right to a gate in the facing hedge. Ahead again, passing ponds to your left, until you eventually come to a sturdy plank over a ditch and a Sandstone Trail marker. Go ahead over this field to a stile by reeded ponds, and ahead again to cross another sturdy plank. Cross three more fields to the right-hand corner of the final one, where you exit via an assortment of stiles and a steel gate. I was quite relieved to reach these as I had shared this last field with a bull - albeit a placid one!

Keep left along the side of a long field, beside a babbling brook which drops down low waterfalls as it is tunnelled under the ground. Turn left at the end over a stile, and immediately right through a self-shutting steel gate. Facing you must be the highest stile in Cheshire, if not in the world! I couldn't resist climbing up the high step ladder and pausing on the platform, which is cunningly placed where the tree trunk divides.

The "highest stile in Cheshire"

Bear to your left up the dry valley, keeping to the higher ground if it is muddy. This will bring you to the by-pass, which you cross. Then follow the telegraph poles for a short way, keeping to the high ground across the field you enter. You soon drop down to the left to pass between sturdy fences and over a stile to a grassy track.

Cross this and keep ahead down the right-hand side of a field to go through a gate into a further field. Bear left to the stile in the far corner of this. Then keep the hedge on your right until you cross another stile, and turn immediately right down a snicket past Tarporley Silver Band hut. When you reach the main street turn right and walk back to the car-park past the Rising Sun, a very old pub with a Preservation Order on it.

SOUTH-EAST OF CHESTER

Brown Knowl
Bunbury
Peckforton
Raw Head

The Pathfinder map for these walks is Farndon, Holt and Tattenhall - Sheet SJ 45/55. Travelling instructions are from Chester. Bunbury is the longest walk, being about seven miles. Raw Head and Peckforton are both about four, and Brown Knowl is around two.

There is a wealth of places to visit in this area to suit all tastes. The grounds of Cholmondeley (pronounced 'Chumly') are over to the east off the A49. The Cholmondeley family have lived there for many generations. The family chapel has a 17th century screen and Commandment Boards. The lovely gardens and grounds are open to the public in the summer months, and the rose garden is particularly impressive.

Beeston Castle is well worth exploring, and Beeston Market is a large cattle market that takes place every Wednesday. Bunbury Mill has been restored to working order. It is open at certain times during the summer months when flour made at the mill can be purchased. At the Candle Factory at Burwardsley you can see the candles being made, and in the summer holidays children can make one themselves.

AROUND BROWN KNOWL

Route: Brown Knowl - Larkton Hill - Maiden Castle - Sandstone Trail - Bickerton Hill

Distance: 2 to 3 miles

Start: The village of Brown Knowl (SJ 497536)

By Car: Take the A41 south from Chester and then turn left onto the A534. This road used to be known as Salters Way. It was the route taken by the salt traders travelling between Nantwich and Chester. At The Copper Mine pub turn right. Park in the vicinity of the telephone box in Brown Knowl village.

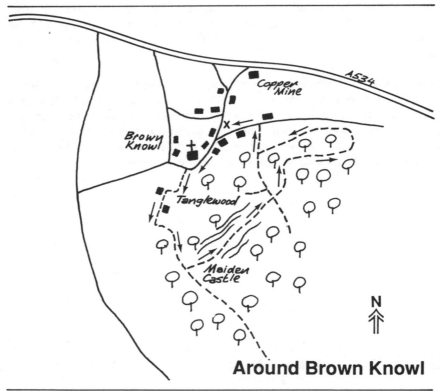

Around Brown Knowl

This walk is a pleasant one for families out for a picnic. There are many places to stop where the views are magnificent, and the children can have fun exploring the woods.

Walk up the hill past the Methodist chapel and take the left fork down the 'No Through Road'. You soon reach a field that may have bullocks in it and turn right. Turn left at the house and continue past Tanglewood. At Larkton Hill go through the posts onto National Trust land.

Continue along a sandy path, bearing left up the hill where it says 'No Horses please'. Keep ahead and an outstanding view over to the Welsh Hills opens out. Bear left again up the hill, joining the Sandstone Trail. The path then continues left up a rocky outcrop and through an area covered with bilberries and heather.

There are severe erosion problems here as you reach the site of the Iron Age fort of Maiden Castle. It was an earth and timber rampart but now mounds of earth are the only evidence of its existence.

Continue to follow the Sandstone Trail markers along the top of the ridge in a north-easterly direction. The level of noise on this walk can vary enormously, from the loud whistling of the wind as you walk along the exposed ridge, to the haven of quietness as you move into the shelter of the wood.

When you reach a crossroads of very sandy tracks go ahead and then round to the left a little further on. As you walk through the woodland here you may notice the witch's broom on many of the silver birch trees. When the trees give way to a field on your left turn down the side of it, walking along the fence at the edge of the wood. The path doubles back the way you have come, but at a lower level along the bottom of the scarp.

You have a good view of the rocky outcrop of Raw Head, aptly-named with its sandstone face exposed to the full force of the weather. The result of wind erosion is plainly evident in its carved out features. Some of the old trees along the bottom of this wood form grotesque shapes, and fallen silver birches have become the habitat of fungi - their brown tops and cream underbellies easy to spot.

When you come to a stile on your right climb over it and go down the path until you cross another stile. Here there may still be a large branch split from a huge beech tree to negotiate, and beech masts in profusion on the ground. Turn left along the country lane back to Brown Knowl and your car.

AROUND BUNBURY

Route: Bunbury church - School Lane - Deanbank Cottages - Beeston Market - Shropshire Union Canal - Bunbury Locks - Calveley - Woodworth Green - Bunbury Mill

Distance: 7 miles

Start: The green by Bunbury church (SJ 570581)

By Car: Take the A51 from Chester. Keep ahead at the A49 and then turn right in Alpraham. As you drive into Bunbury park near the church beside the green in Bowes Gate Road.

Walk back to the church and turn right over a stile into the cemetery. Early in the year snowdrops form bright patches in the grass. Cross an iron stepladder stile and make for a stile across the field. Turn left up the road and then right after passing a chapel - now used for a different purpose.

Walk down the side of the field into a little valley and across a stile. Keep to the high ground across the next field until you come to a signpost and drop down to cross the River Gowy. With the hedge on your right, walk along to the next stile and then walk diagonally across the next field to the stile in the corner. Two strips of pine trees shelter this field where birds swoop and whirl. Bear right to face the busy A49 and walk round two sides of this field until you come to a stile out of it. The stile immediately ahead has an old boundary stone beside it and you then go through a cobbled snicket to a track that leads onto School Lane. Turn right and then right again to walk down the A49 for a short way, passing Yew Tree House with its mullioned windows and ornamental owls.

After passing Beeston Gate Farm, its gables and honeycomb windows worth a second glance, go over the stile towards Beeston Castle. Keep to your left in the field. There may be sheep lambing if it is springtime, so keep a dog closely under control on its lead. There is a stile in the fence on your left just before the end of this field. Cross it and turn right. Keep

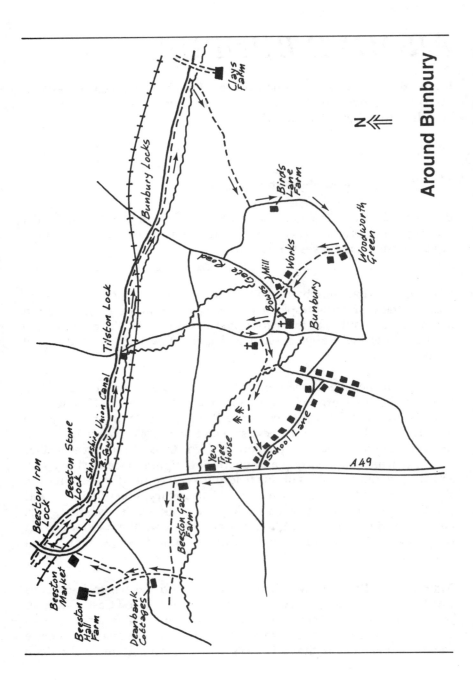

Around Bunbury

along here until you cross a further stile by a pond. Keep ahead near the hedge until you come to another stile onto a grassy track. Here, you turn right to Deanbank Cottages. Cross the country lane and go over the cattle grid and down the farm road towards Beeston Hall Farm. Turn right over a stile along here and the path drops down through a new plantation of evergreens. It then skirts the next field before crossing a final meadow and taking you over a stile into Beeston cattle market (the Smithfield of the north). This is held every Wednesday and is well worth a visit.

Turn left along the A49 to walk under the railway bridge, cross the River Gowy, and then drop down off the road onto the towpath of the Shropshire Union canal. Turn right to go under the substantial stone bridge and pass Beeston Iron Lock and Beeston Stone Lock. It is easy to see how they each got their name. Farther along, Tilston Lock is interesting with its horse path and the converted miller's house. If you are weary, you can cut back to your car, either from here, or from Bunbury Locks which are worth seeing.

Keeping along the towpath you next come to an iron railway bridge made at Roodee Foundry, Chester, before reaching the staircase locks at Bunbury. Dartline boatbuilders operate here, too, and you can often see a new craft being built or, in the summer, the hirers of narrow boats preparing to embark.

Continue along the canal to do the longer walk, and you see a derelict earthwork with brick-built tunnels and archways - perhaps a relic from the last war? You next pass a sludge lagoon, and then drop down off the towpath over a stile, before reaching the next bridge and Clays Farm. Walk across the field to another stile and a log bridge over the River Gowy. Follow the line of telegraph poles all the way across the next field, which is ridged, and leave it by way of a stile and a plank. Keep to the right of the telegraph poles across the next field to cross two stiles separated by a planked bridge out of it. Keep the barbed wire fence on your left as you cross the next field, and you will soon come to a way out of it beside an oak tree in the corner. Cross this field diagonally, noting the line of trees along the lost hedge where you dip down. It is another very ridged field and you pass a pond on your way over it.

Cross a stile between a gate and a trough and turn left along the road.

Bunbury Locks.

Along here a large radio telescope comes into view. After passing Bird's Lane Farm, the sandstone tower of Bunbury Church indicates that you are nearing the end of your walk.

When you reach the tiny hamlet of Woodworth Green turn right at the footpath sign that leads you over a stile. After passing the two houses strike out across the field, making for the gate which lies between an oak tree and a telegraph pole. Go through this into the next field, where you skirt a crescent of rabbit holes in the sandy bank.

Pass the sewage works on your right and drop down to the stile. This brings you over rough ground to a gap in the fence where there used to be a small gate. Go through this and turn left onto the road.

The restoration of Bunbury Mill was carried out by the North West Water Authority in 1974. The machinery is now in working order and the mill is open to the public on certain days throughout the summer months, when you can see it operating. Walk past the door in the wall of the upper storey. In the old days, sacks full of flour were passed out of this onto a cart below. You can then go down the steps formed by an old millstone to read the rhyme on the mill door which exhorts the miller to be kind and honest.

You have a choice here. You can either walk up past the cottages on the old cobbles to turn left along the road back to the church and your car. Or, you can go through the gate into the field at the far side of the circular car-park. Walk up the field towards the church, and there is a stile in the corner which takes you back to your car.

AROUND PECKFORTON

Route: Beeston Castle - Sandstone Trail - Peckforton Woods - Willis's Wood - Beeston Village

Distance: 4 miles

Start: The Sandstone Trail notice board at Beeston Castle (SJ 540590)

By Car: Take the A51 from Chester. Turn right at the A49 and follow the signs to Beeston Castle which are very clear. Beeston Castle is well worth a visit, and you park in the car-park there.

Beeston Castle was built in 1220 as a military stronghold and it has a turbulent history. Beeston Crag provides an ideal position for a fortress, its jagged precipice rising 300 feet above the surrounding countryside. There was also a never-failing supply of fresh water from a well 370 feet deep in the courtyard. This is reputed to have treasure buried at the bottom of it. A labyrinth of caves provide an ideal venue for games of hide-and-seek for youngsters not so fond of sight-seeing!

Elizabethan Farmhouse.

158

Beeston Castle.

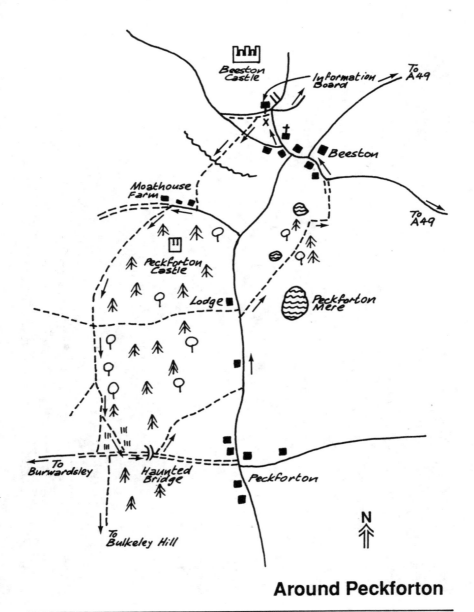

Around Peckforton

Walk to the Sandstone Trail information board. As you face the castle entrance it is over to the left. Castle Snacks provide a variety of refreshments from a caravan sited here for much of the year. Follow the Sandstone Trail through the snicket, walking beside the wall for a short way and then bearing left. Walk down through the wood on a soft carpet of pine needles until you cross the stile onto the road. Cross over and take the path opposite, which unfolds ahead across fields to Peckforton Woods.

Turn right at the platform stile along a country lane to pass Moathouse Farm, with its roughly-hewn sandstone outbuildings, old byre and Elizabethan farmhouse dwarfed by its massive brick chimney. A mineral spring, noted for the purity of its water, surfaces in the private grounds here. Turn left through the gate into Peckforton Estate woods, still following the Sandstone Trail towards Bulkeley Hill. Forestry and pheasant rearing still take place on the estate and these birds may strut across the path. It is a peaceful place, where the wind soughs through the branches, and snatches of nearby fields appear where the trees peter out.

At the first junction continue towards Bulkeley Hill. The aromatic smell of newly-sawn timber may follow you from the clearing here. The roofs of Higher Burwardsley can be seen. Its well-known inn, the Pheasant, often causes walkers of the Trail to deviate awhile! In the distance the craggy, sandstone cliffs of Raw Head come into view. Where the track drops down to the right turn left up a little path to follow the Sandstone Trail towards Bulkeley Hill for the last time on this walk. The path climbs diagonally up the side of the hill. Round growths, like warts, plague the oak trees near the top.

Climb over the stile at the summit and your way is ahead, leaving the Sandstone Trail which turns right. This right-of-way, which cuts off a corner, has only been opened recently, and you pass immediately through a new plantation of Christmas trees. Once you have climbed another stile there is a wilder area of gorse, bracken and bramble. You may feel as if you are on top of the world here! Reeds, marshland and moss finish the short cut. This part is reminiscent of the marshland setting for The Hound of the Baskervilles!

When you meet a main track by a small pond turn left and you soon pass under the Haunted Bridge. At the second turning to the left walk to the signpost even though there is a notice saying 'Strictly Private'. From here you will see the hidden pathway that runs parallel with the road for a short way, and then cuts clearly over stiles and fields down to the road. Turn left along the road and you will see Peckforton Mere, and pass Garden Cottage, made of sandstone and still maintaining a cobbled drive. Just before you pass the lodge of Peckforton Castle, confronted by an old oak tree, turn right over a stile towards Beeston Moss and Bunbury. Don't panic, I am not sending you quite that far!

Veer left across this field with Beeston and Peckforton castles standing sentinel on their respective hills like father and son. Peckforton Castle is really a sham. It was built in the mid-19th century from locally-quarried sandstone by Lord Tollemache. Modelled on a Norman castle it was to be his country seat.

The line of four trees ahead are all that remains of the hedgerow that once divided this field. Pass through the middle of these trees - to the right of the tree surrounded by molehills. As you breast the crown of the hill you will see the stile ahead beside a gate. Honking balefully, geese may rise from the ponds that have formed here.

Go over the stile and into the wood to walk along a broad, grassy ride. Leave the wood over another stile and bear right to a stile that gives access onto a cart-track. Here you turn left and walk to the farm where you turn right onto the road. Take the next turn left to pass an old farm cottage, built on a cruck (curved) frame. Most of the cottages in Beeston date from the 17th century and there are numerous examples of the typical 'magpie' dwellings in this area. Turn left again past another old cottage, right at another, and right again. You then pass a converted chapel and soon arrive back at the car-park.

AROUND RAW HEAD

Route: Gallantry Bank - Tower Wood - Sandstone Trail - Raw Head - Bulkeley Hill

Distance: 4 miles

Start: The old chimney at the top of Gallantry Bank (SJ 518542)

By Car: Take the A41 south from Chester and turn left onto the A534. After going up Gallantry Bank and passing Gallantry Bank Cottage, park in the gravel lay-by opposite the tall chimney. This belonged to the pumping house of a Copper Mine that operated here in the 18th century. Alas, there was not enough copper found to make it economically viable.

Cross the road and go up the 'No Through Road', passing the chimney. You soon come to a signpost to the Sandstone Trail and turn left into a Wildlife Conservation Area. Notice the caves set back into the hillside here. There are many stories about the caves in this area, which are thought to have been the hide-outs for bands of robbers and highwaymen. Keep along the fence, crossing the stream and climbing up the hill. The narrow stiles are aptly named squeezer stiles.

Turn right onto the Sandstone Trail at the edge of Tower Wood. The signpost says to Rawhead and Beeston. You can see Bulkeley Hill, which you visit on the second part of this walk, as the path follows the edge of the wood, and the view gets better as you rise higher.

You come to the deep gully of Musket's Hole with a huge bastion of sandstone facing you. Notice the honeycomb effect of wind erosion on the layers of rock. The path works its way round the head of this gully and up rough-hewn steps in the rock.

The trig point at Raw Head comes into sight. It is the highest point of the Sandstone Trail at 746 feet above sea level (227 metres). It is well worth stopping when this is reached to admire the outstanding view which stretches over the Cheshire plain as far as the Welsh Hills.

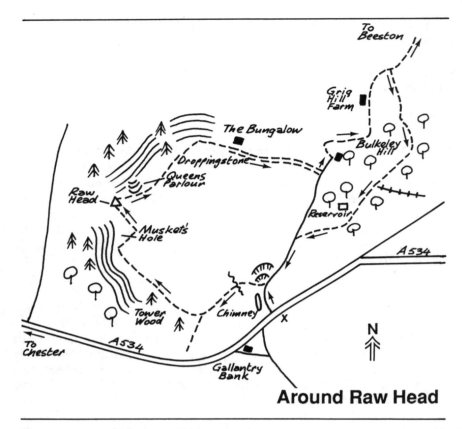

Around Raw Head

Keep along the Sandstone Trail on the top path, which goes along the edge of the scarp by the field fence. There is a spectacular sandstone cave below the path here, although it is a scramble down to reach it. It is called the Queen's Parlour and is thought to be the result of local men excavating for sand.

After crossing a stile a large rock overhangs the path and the smooth slopes of Burwardsley Hill are clearly outlined ahead. Cross another stile to descend well-made wooden steps, and then continue to a gently dripping rock overhang. This is where a spring surfaces and is known locally as the Droppingstone - although Drippingstone would be a better description of it. Soon after this a criss-cross stile brings you out of the Wildlife Conservation Area.

Turn right past The Bungalow and keep on until you turn left at a T-junction towards the Peckforton Gap. You soon turn left again, down a track that gives access to walkers and residents' vehicles only. As you round a bend along here it is better to avoid contact with the large gorse bushes.

After passing Grig Hill Farm turn right at a handrail with a Sandstone Trail sign. You are now going up onto Bulkeley Hill. Much of the landscape of this hill is composed of silver birches sticking out of bracken, heather and bilberry. Climb up sandstone steps and the path winds round to the right. As you gain height views over Peckforton Mere and the north-east open up through the trees.

Keep along the edge of the wood and you soon come to a weirdly-shaped tree, ideal for swinging on. Just beside it a narrow, one-track tramway drops steeply down the side of the hill. This was built to transport heavy materials when a water pipeline was being built to tap the reservoirs on the hilltop. Rainwater percolates through the porous sandstone and then collects when it reaches a layer of non-porous clay. This provides enough water for the villages of south-west Cheshire.

Other trees offer ideal climbing facilities and there is a flat rock from which to view Bulkeley village. It looks like a scene from Toyland so far below. Go through the gateway in an old iron fence. To the right is one of the reservoirs mentioned earlier. Drop down the hill here until you come to a signpost where you turn right to Rawhead and Larkton Hill over a stile. Cross a further stile and turn left along the road, which winds down the hill, taking you back to the lay-by and your car.

Also of Interest:

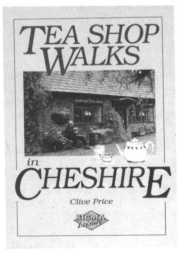

EAST CHESHIRE WALKS: FROM PEAK TO PLAIN
Graham Beech
The definitive guide to walking in East Cheshire is now in its third edition - and still outselling all other local walking guides! Completely updated and revised, the 39 walks cover 250 miles, including a 20-mile challenge route. £6.95

BEST PUB WALKS IN CHESHIRE
Jen Darling
This is the second edition of the most comprehensive pub walks guide to the county. Fully revised for the millennium! £6.95

CHESHIRE WALKS WITH CHILDREN
Nick Lambert
This was the first in our "walks with children" series and has quickly become a firm favourite. Things to look out for and questions to answer along the way make it an entertaining book for young and old alike. £6.95

BEST TEA SHOP WALKS IN CHESHIRE
Clive Price
Cheshire is the epitome of tea shop country - "...a winning blend of scenic strolls and tasty tea shops" CHESHIRE LIFE. £6.95

A YEAR OF WALKS: CHESHIRE
Clive Price
Walk in harmony with the changing seasons. Routes from 4 to 12 miles with something special to offer for the particular time of year: Swettenham's Daffodil Dell, Audlem's canal boats in the summer, winter birds along the wilderness of the Dee Estuary or Shutlingsloe transformed by snow. £7.95

EAST CHESHIRE MYTHS & LEGENDS
Doug Pickford
"An author who knows his stuff; would make a delightful present; an abundance of pictures" CHESTER CHRONICLE. £5.95

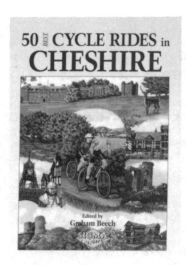
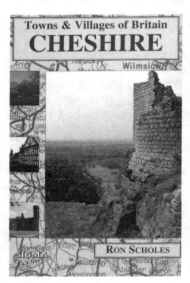